D&O 101:
Understanding Directors & Officers Liability Insurance

A Holistic Approach

Larry Goanos

Wells Media Group is a business-to-business media company with a focus on the property/casualty insurance industry. Our brands include Insurance Journal, Claims Journal, Carrier Management, Insurance Journal's Academy of Insurance and MyNewMarkets.com. We report news, provide access to resources, education, and information to build communities to inform and connect our audiences.

"When you learn, teach. When you get, give."

Maya Angelou (1928 – 2014)

Contents

Foreword

The great American jurist Oliver Wendell Holmes, Jr. once said that "All life is an experiment." We test our circumstances as they are presented to us and make our field assessments as conditions unfold. What's left at the end is experience.

Through a long and varied career as a coverage attorney, underwriting manager, broker and insurance subsidiary president, Larry Goanos, this book's author, has accumulated an abundance of experience.

As this book's very existence demonstrates, over the course of a long and varied career, one not only acquires and develops the precise skills of technique, but one also acquires the less precise but arguably more important skills of instinct and intuition. Over time, one learns not only the importance of listening attentively to that small internal voice, one learns how to make that inner voice speak.

These observations are true about life in general. They are also true to the very specific topic of this book, which is D&O Insurance underwriting. When it comes to D&O underwriting, precise technique is indispensable. However, it is not sufficient. As Larry says in an early chapter, D&O underwriting is both a science and an art. Larry advocates what he calls a "holistic" approach to D&O underwriting. In this approach, instinct matters as well as technique. It is all about developing – and then listening to – that inner voice.

Like Larry, I have worn many hats. Most recently, I have been wearing the broker's hat, after having served as a coverage attorney and then as an underwriter. When I first became a broker, I had an unexpectedly educational experience observing other underwriters engage in the front line underwriting process. Although there are many excellent underwriters out there, I was surprised and troubled to see a few who were not, shall we say, excellent.

Early in my tenure as a broker, I was working on a public company D&O Insurance renewal. The renewal presented one issue and one issue only. The company had a balloon debt payment due in February and it did not have the resources to make the payment. If the company failed to make the payment, it would likely go out of business. In anticipation of the renewal meeting with the underwriters, I spent several hours with the CFO, refining the response to the inevitable question about the company's looming debt obstacle.

As it turned out, I could have saved the time and effort. Not one of the underwriters asked about the debt. They asked a bunch of questions about how the quarter was turning out and various issues involving vendor and customer arrangements, none of which could possibly matter if the company failed to make the upcoming debt payment.

The company's D&O Insurance program ultimately renewed with an overall ten percent premium decrease. The following March, after the company failed to make the balloon payment, the company went bankrupt. Shortly before the bankruptcy, shareholders filed a securities class action. In addition, the trustee in bankruptcy filed breach of fiduciary duty claims against the company's directors and officers. Between defense costs and settlements, almost the entire D&O Insurance tower was consumed.

At the time of the renewal meeting, I wanted to say to each of the underwriters "Every single one of you gets an 'F'." I restrained myself at the time; the underwriters got their report card eventually. The underwriters, referring only to their standard list of underwriting issues, asked a multitude of questions but failed to learn what mattered, because they had failed at the outset to see the company for what it was.

The point is that D&O underwriting requires more than a checklist approach. Effective D&O underwriting requires both a technical understanding of an account's characteristics as well as a grasp of a company's overall risk profile.

Throughout the book, Larry interjects the phrase "that brings to mind a story." Larry has a seemingly endless supply of stories, carefully assembled here to underscore a long list of underwriting lessons, all calculated to try to identify what goes into developing that deeper appreciation of underwriting risk.

There is another important lesson that Larry's book embodies, perhaps implicitly – and that is that as you make your way through your career, one of the most valuable things you can do is to develop a network of industry friends and colleagues. And when it comes to developing a network, Larry has achieved master status.

Because of Larry's experience and because of his vast array of industry friends (many of whom provide their own advice in the book's final section), Larry has been able to assemble a book that does a rare and valuable thing – it both educates and entertains. Even the book's thorough explanation of the basic terms of the D&O Insurance policy is entertaining, which is an achievement in and of itself.

Though Larry's approach is personal and anecdotal, he also provides a great detailed overview of all of the basic technical concepts involved with D&O Insurance underwriting, from financial analysis to the assessment of company management. The book also addresses perennial issues, such as limits selection, retentions, coinsurance and much more besides.

Larry's book represents a valuable resource for anyone involved with the D&O Insurance industry or who want to try to understand how it works at the basic transactional level. The book not only provides a useful introduction to the D&O Insurance underwriting process, but it also provides an insider's look at the way things actually work in the trenches.

It is obvious that Larry had a lot of fun writing this book. The rest of us get to have the pleasure of reading it.

Kevin M. LaCroix, Esq.
Executive Vice President
R-T ProExec, A Division of R-T Specialty, LLC
Author, The D&O Diary Blog

Preface

I wrote this book to share some important lessons I've learned during 20-plus years of dealing with Directors and Officers Liability Insurance ("D&O") as an insurance coverage attorney, an underwriting manager, a broker and an insurance company subsidiary president. I'm hopeful that my experiences are helpful as you make your way in the D&O Insurance industry. In this book, I will talk about not just "academic" facts, such as the significance of earnings per share or the role of independent directors, but also "softer" facts, things revealed through real-word lessons – D&O in the trenches.

The purpose of this book is to provide useful information that will help you *right now*, whether you are an experienced insurance professional considering a move into the D&O world or an insurance student or new hire interested in gaining "inside knowledge" about D&O Insurance. D&O veterans might even learn a thing or two from the following pages, which are chock full of industry nuggets. Just one tip found in this book has the potential to save an insurance company millions of dollars or, conversely, help an insured collect millions on a claim that wouldn't otherwise have been covered. That may seem to be a melodramatic statement, but it's true!

Please keep in mind, however (Warning: Disclaimer Ahead!), that I do not provide any legal, accounting or tax advice in this book. I strongly recommend that anyone seeking such advice should consult a qualified professional in the appropriate field. Every situation is unique and needs to be analyzed in light of a number of specific factors. Translation: Don't sue me based on anything you read in this book, its buyer beware!

When I began my career in D&O Insurance, a resource such as this would have been a godsend – a valuable reference to which I would have continually returned. It might also have saved me a few embarrassing moments. One that comes to mind occurred early in my insurance career when I first heard the term "around-the-clock reinstatement." I knew it had something to do with a policy's limit of liability, but I didn't know exactly what it meant. And, making a common rookie mistake, I was too embarrassed to ask anyone for guidance [I strongly believe that the only dumb question is the one not asked!] Thus, I assumed, incorrectly, that an around-the-clock reinstatement afforded insureds the right to call a carrier at any time of night or day to get their limit of liability reinstated after a loss. I have plenty of additional examples along these lines, but I'll spare myself the public embarrassment. Here's a bit more about my background to give you a better understanding of the origins of my insights.

Like many in the professional lines insurance world, of which D&O Insurance is an important part, I fell into the field by happenstance. I'm sure that's not an unfamiliar scenario to many of you who also arrived in this profession after receiving a shove from the Hand of Fate. Despite my haphazard entrance into professional lines insurance – I answered a blind want ad in the **New York Law Journal** that led to a job with one of AIG's primary outside D&O law firms – I could scarcely be happier with the outcome.

At first, I didn't even know D&O stood for "Directors and Officers." I had been mildly unhappy working as a legal editor in Manhattan for a little more than a year after graduating from law school, so I decided to try practicing law. Answering the **NYLJ** ad was, for me, as random as going to a party and running into cousin Evan from Chubb or college friend Claudia from Marsh and fortuitously landing an interview.

D'Amato & Lynch, the law firm behind that **NYLJ** ad, gave me my first taste of professional lines insurance. It was a wonderful place for a newbie to cut his teeth. Co-founder George D'Amato was still running the firm in those days. The term "ironfisted" doesn't quite describe George's management style; I'd say "titanium" more closely fit the bill. Nonetheless, being a shrewd businessman, as well as top-flight lawyer, George surrounded himself with great minds from which a neophyte like me could learn. Lawyers such as Richard George (R.I.P.), Bob Gilroy, Luke Lynch, Jr., Ken Sagat, Harry Arnold, Barbara Seymour, Bob Lang, MaryJo Barry, Scott Schaffer, Neal Glazer, Steven Gladstone, Brian Kristiansen, John FitzSimons, Susanne (Mast) Murray, Sam Paniccia and others who I'm sure I'm forgetting, freely shared their insights and experience.

    I left D'Amato & Lynch after two years to work for William "Bill" Cotter at Parker, Coulter, Daley & White in Boston, a firm that did work similar to D'Amato & Lynch's but for a greater array of clients. Bill (may he rest in peace) had a brilliant legal mind, significant insurance experience and was a great person from whom to learn. Bill also surrounded himself with very talented lawyers such as Chris Betke, Brian O'Connell, Joe O'Neil, Emily Coughlin, Joe Smick, Kevin Cain, Bob Gill and Mark Rosen. Three years later, in 1994, I returned to New York to become Chief Underwriting Officer for the Financial Institutions Group of AIG subsidiary National Union Fire Insurance Company of Pittsburgh, Pa. ("National Union.") This was the start of a fun and challenging ride in professional lines insurance that would take me to jobs at Marsh in San Francisco, back to AIG in New York and then ACE, Marsh (again) and PIA/Houston Casualty. Currently, I run my own professional lines insurance consulting business, Andros Risk Services, LLC.

    My insurance career has afforded me the good fortune of working for, and with, many wise and talented people. Besides those named above, I learned a great deal from Lena Mkhitarian, Robert Omahne, Jack Flug, Mike Mitrovic, Greg Flood, Lisa Doherty, Judy Lindenmayer (R.I.P.), John Lupica, Dave Lupica, Tim O'Donnell, Walter S. Tomenson, Jr., Tom Vietor (R.I.P.), LouAnn Layton, Dean Klisura, Hank Whiting Adriaan Schieferdecker, Dick Barquist, K.C. Kidder, Carmelo

Casella, Merritt Fabel, Tom Zacharopoulos, Mike Schell, Cory Moulton, Bill Brown and a host of others. If I listed everyone, you'd fall asleep, but the omitted people know who they are and, hopefully, how grateful I am.

I've been involved with small accounts, to be sure, but most of my experience comes from dealing with Fortune 1000 companies. Underwriting professional lines products and working as an insurance broker for organizations such as Bank of America, Tyson Foods, J.P. Morgan Chase, Home Depot, Fannie Mae, Freddie Mac, UPS, Fidelity Investments, Boeing, Chevron, Wells Fargo, Apple, Google, Citigroup, Lehman Brothers and Goldman Sachs, to name just a handful, has provided me with countless insights and lessons. I hope in this book to share some of the more valuable ones.

Our industry, which I love, has some glaring deficiencies, I'll admit. One of the most notable is the dearth of professional lines-specific training materials. Ask any newly-minted insurance broker how extensively professional lines were covered in his broker training course, or the licensing exam itself, and, invariably, the answer will be "Very little." But that same broker, who within a year of starting in the business may be working on a Fortune 500 company's D&O program, will be able to tell you if a trailer parked in a driveway is covered under a homeowner's policy for damage from a windstorm. The insurance industry does not always traffic in logic.

I never worked at Chubb, but my impression is that it's one of the few companies that provides ample professional lines training to inexperienced hires. (I don't know why I'm complimenting Chubb, with its comprehensive training program it will probably have no need to buy copies of this book!) Many other companies' training consists of merely dumping a bunch of insurance policies and applications on a neophyte's desk with instructions to start reading.

The goal of this book is to provide insights into D&O underwriting – both rudimentary and advanced – while approaching the field as *both* an art and a science. I'll attempt to illuminate these points with a fair sprinkling of "real world war stories." I know what you're thinking, but please don't yawn just yet. I did my best to employ only relevant and interesting tales. To me, true tales from the front lines of insurance help bring to life the principles of underwriting and the overall coverage itself. I was originally going to try to cover all professional lines in this volume, but I thought better of it; such a work would've taken a long time to write and it would be much too long for most busy professionals to read in any reasonable amount of time.

In my first book, *Claims Made & Reported: A Journey Through D&O, E&O and Other Professional Lines of Insurance* [Soho Publishing: New York 2008, 376 pages], which was something of an oral history of professional lines insurance, I recited a line I'd heard from a senior manager at AIG during an orientation session for new employees. He said "Welcome to AIG. Our philosophy here is to just throw you into the water right away to see if you sink or swim. If you sink, you're done. If you swim, we throw bricks at you."

And, boy, he wasn't kidding!

Of course, there's something to be said for learning on the job and gaining experience rapidly in a baptism by fire. Sometimes you just have to go for it. Speaking of which, after *Claims Made & Reported* was published in 2008, I rolled the dice and sent a copy to Warren Buffett, hoping he'd like the book and provide a complimentary quote we could use to help promote and sell the book. (100 percent of the proceeds of *Claims Made & Reported* are split among four charities.) Mr. Buffett's exceedingly nice and professional assistant, Deb Bosanek, called me a few days later to say Mr. Buffett appreciated the free book but that he wouldn't have time to read it. I was disappointed, obviously, but also astounded – and appreciative – that Mr. Buffett would take the time to have his assistant call me. However, I was astounded to a far greater degree when, eight months later, I opened an email from Mr. Buffett telling me he had read the book, enjoyed it and hoped that his insurance managers would all get a copy, too. He also noted that I was wrong when I wrote in the book that he'd never read it, thus proving he really did read it. I've exchanged a few emails with Mr. Buffett since then, and he has always been exceedingly kind, gracious and down to earth. Yes, the public image really is accurate.

I'm going to send a complimentary copy of this book to Mr. Buffett, as well, but we all know he's extremely busy and no doubt won't have time to read it. (Who am I kidding? He'll see right through this feeble attempt at reverse psychology.)

That's OK though, I'll still look forward to the phone call that I hope to get from Ms. Bosanek.

A stylistic point: Readers may tire of seeing the words "generally," "normally," "usually," "typically" and similar terms, but because of the wide variety of policy wordings, industry protocols and other factors, it's very difficult to set forth a lot of hard-and-fast rules that are *always* true in the world of D&O Insurance. Just about all of the principles that I set forth in this book must be viewed through the prism of the actual facts and circumstances of any particular situation. So please forgive the repetition, including this repetition of a disclaimer; I generally thank you!

A few final notes of appreciation.

Heartfelt thanks go out to James Drinkwater, Richard Fernandez, Sarah Ruble, David Lewison, Bill Dixon, Andrew Pritchard, Dan O'Connor, Mike Borghesi, Jessica Brown and all of their talented colleagues at AmWINS who supported my consulting firm, Andros Risk Services, during the writing of this book, including by commissioning me to write articles about, and provide training to their colleagues on, various insurance topics. I'd also like to thank Lee Lerner who used his superb editing skills to make the book's first draft much better. Michael J. Healey provided astute editorial insights and direction. Mitch Dunford, Barbara Whiffen, Allison Steinkamp, and Derence Walk of Wells Media Group also have my gratitude for their great work in support of this project. In my first book, I forgot to mention Mike Kambos, so I'm including his name here. Now he's obligated to buy multiple copies of this book. Shameless, I know. And I tip my hat to the members of FETA, a world-class organization.

I was sincerely honored to have Kevin LaCroix write the Foreword to this book. He did an outstanding job, not surprisingly. Kevin is the author of the highly-respected blog **The D&O Diary** (www.dandodiary.com). Kevin's blog is widely known as one of the most authoritative, well-written and comprehensive sources of D&O information in the industry. If you're not familiar with The D&O Diary, I'd urge you to visit the site, it's well worth your time.

And, last but certainly not least, I'd like to thank my awesome wife, Ilona, and my wonderful stepchildren Kathryn, Laura and Eric. Ilona has been the love of my life since the first day I met her in college. She supported and encouraged my efforts as I wrote, and I could not have produced this book without her.

I hope you enjoy reading D&O 101 and that you learn a few things along the way. Six very worthy charities will each receive 15 percent of my share of this book's profits. Hopefully, you'll feel good about your purchase supporting these six great organizations (information about each appears at the back of the book).

Finally, if you read within these pages anything that you believe needs clarifying or correcting, or if there's something you think should be in a second edition, please feel free to email me at **lgoanos@androsriskservices.com**.

I sincerely thank you for buying this book.

Introduction

There's an old saying in the insurance industry that's particularly applicable to carriers: "*Nobody likes surprises.*" This, at least in part, is why I believe some people would prefer to reduce D&O Insurance underwriting to exact formulas with little room for divergence. It downplays the role of experience and intuition and other intangibles in the underwriting process and makes underwriters more fungible. It also creates the illusion that D&O underwriting is predictable and will give rise to very few surprises. There are a number of reasons for this thinking, in my opinion. Here's one: When an insurer loses a group of underwriters to a rival, it doesn't want to admit it just parted ways with some difficult-to-replace assets. Rather, that company would much prefer to release a statement to analysts and shareholders saying something like: "We base our underwriting on a precise and proprietary formula and the loss of these underwriters will not affect the quality of our underwriting in any significant way."

Yeah, sure, we buy that.

Another reason: When there are literally tens of millions or even hundreds of millions of dollars at stake, most insurance executives don't want to think that intuition, personal experience, personal relationships and other intangibles play a meaningful role in the fate of that capital.

Many years ago, when I was at National Union, I wrote an email to our underwriters in which I referred to the "art" of professional lines underwriting. I said that underwriting our products was not simply a scientific process relying solely upon formulas in analyzing various metrics – although there's certainly a substantial amount of that involved – and that various intangibles needed to be considered as well.

The next day, Evan Greenberg, at the time a high-ranking AIG executive, was moved to write a company-wide email in the aftermath of a large loss that had erupted from a shoddily underwritten account (note: it wasn't in my group!). He reminded everyone that underwriting is a science and NOT an art and should be approached as such. It took a third of a nanosecond for underwriters to begin charging into my office to point out that my underwriting philosophy was at odds with one of the company's senior leaders. The fact that Evan, for whom I have great respect and admiration, has been the highly successful CEO of ACE for some time now and I'm merely running a one-man consulting business, to me, should not be construed as confirmation of the validity of his opinion!

Make no mistake: My premise is not that D&O Insurance underwriting is strictly a seat-of-the-pants, gut-feeling enterprise. To the contrary; empirical evidence – analysis of numbers, formulas, ratios and other cold, hard facts – plays a central role in D&O underwriting. However, I believe these concrete considerations must be viewed through a prism that allows for instinct, experience, "gut feelings" and other "soft" considerations to infuse the underwriting process as well. At least with respect to larger accounts, to be sure. And many of these intuitive factors can be incorporated into the underwriting process for high-volume, "low-touch" smaller accounts as well.

Here are three examples to illustrate my belief that outside-the-box underwriting has its place in professional lines insurance.

The first occurred while I was at AIG. A fairly new underwriter came into my office to review an Investment Management Insurance account with me. He was seeking authority to quote a $10 million limit of liability. We reviewed all of the standard metrics and discussed claims history (none) and other traditional factors. Finally, at the end of the meeting, just before I was about to grant him the requisite authority and sign off on his quote sheet, I said, "Is there anything else of significance that I should know about this account?"

"Oh, yeah, I guess so," he said. "This company is under indictment in Connecticut for allegedly bribing the state treasurer to use their firm to advise the state pension plan."

"Are you serious?" I asked. "Why didn't you tell me this right at the beginning of this review?"

"Well there was no place to put this information on the underwriting worksheet, so I didn't know how important it was," he replied.

Incredibly, that's an absolutely true story, as all in this book are.

The second example occurred a few years later. One of the country's largest retailers had submitted an excess D&O

application to us through its broker, one of the large "alpha house" insurance brokerages. The broker was pressuring us to quote, in a fairly short time frame, the layer of liability of $10 million in excess of $50 million. The underwriter brought in the file for my review. This was a high-profile account. The broker had already made a call to a senior underwriting executive above me, asking for a favor in getting the account quoted quickly and at the price the broker sought.

In reviewing the file, I saw a number of red flags that did not sit well with me. One of the most prominent of which was that the company had hired the rock band Kiss to perform at a store opening. This, to me, seemed wasteful. I could somewhat understand splashing out to hire Kiss for a national manager meeting, or perhaps even a large regional managers meeting, but for a single store opening? I thought to myself, "Wal-Mart is the paradigm of an efficient retail company. It would never waste money on anything like this. I don't think this company is well run. It's not keeping an adequate focus on the bottom line as Wal-Mart would."

I must emphasize that the Kiss factor was not the only reason I didn't like this risk. There were a number of more traditional considerations weighing against the account as well (e.g. sales trending downward, large backlog of inventory gathering dust, etc.), but the hiring of Kiss sealed the deal in my mind. It was, if you'll forgive me for this bad pun, the Kiss of Death for the account. (I'll pause while you groan.)

So, I directed the underwriter to issue a declination. Within an hour, the senior underwriting executive who had previously been called by the broker phoned me from his office at company headquarters to ask me to explain why we had declined the account. The irate broker had called the executive to voice his extreme displeasure with my decision. I explained a number of the tangible factors that led to my decision. I also mentioned the hiring of Kiss. I can't say if the Kiss Factor had any impact on the executive, but, apparently, something did since he said, "OK, you guys have good reasons for doing what you're doing. I'm going to support your judgment. I'll call the broker and tell him that we're sticking with our declination."

I know it's going to seem like I'm patting myself on the back here, but about six months later that company got hit with multiple securities class actions. The suits alleged a number of things, poor management of company assets among them. The hiring of Kiss to play at a store opening wasn't specifically mentioned, but it was there between the lines – in my mind anyway!

There's a saying in the insurance industry, *"Sometimes, the biggest wins are the accounts you don't write."*[1] This particular account fell into that category for sure.

The third example occurred about a year after the Kiss situation. An underwriter and I attended a group meeting with the CFO of a tech company that was about to go public. There was a lot of buzz surrounding this company and they were building a big D&O program to go along with their very large

---

[1] Sometimes, when an underwriter purposely allows a bad account to get away, they'll say something along the lines of "*I'm happy to roll that grenade into my competitor's camp.*"

IPO. Everything the CFO said sounded kosher except for one thing that stuck in my craw: The founders of the company, still in charge, had created two classes of stock for the IPO, an "A" class for the general public, and a "B" class for themselves which had super voting rights. (I recall it being something like 10 votes for each B share and only one vote for each A share although I'm not 100% positive at this point.) One of the founders (both were still in their 20s, I believe) had recently been quoted as saying they wanted to be in charge of the company for a long time.

As a D&O underwriter, you don't like management declaring that they're entrenching themselves in power in any way. Theoretically, if they are doing a bad job, senior executives should be willing to step aside, not dig themselves further into their positions. I just had a bad feeling about the whole situation on this account. What they were doing wasn't illegal or unethical, I just didn't like it. So I told the underwriter to decline to quote a D&O policy for this company. Despite significant pressure from the broker to quote the business, we stood our ground. I also thought the IPO was overpriced and that the company's long-term prospects weren't absolutely sterling given all the competitors they had at the time. Plenty of other D&O carriers, however, lined up to write the account.

Well, I was right – and wrong. More wrong than right, though, by a long shot.

While the company did get sued eventually over the voting rights of the two classes of shares at some point (I don't remember how it turned out), the stock took off like a rocket and continued to grow exponentially over the years. I'm sure that the D&O carriers on that original program made a lot of money over the years if they stayed on the account. And the company has become one of the tech world's greatest successes to date.

In fact, I wish I had bought the stock shortly after the IPO. The company was Google. If you don't know much about Google, you can Google it.

Just to set the record straight, despite my seemingly boastful stories, I'm not saying my underwriting record is spotless; I've had my share of accounts "go pear-shaped" on me, as our English friends would say.[2] You'll hear more about some of the disasters later.

What I am saying is that consideration of intangibles, something that wouldn't ordinarily show up in the four corners of a standard underwriting worksheet and can't easily be plugged into a rating formula, can make a difference. For example, to the best of my knowledge, the question "Did the company ever hire Kiss to play at a store opening?" does not appear on any carrier's standard underwriting worksheet (although it might after people read this).

In the pages that follow, I attempt to provide some of my insights into both the art *and* science of D&O Insurance underwriting, seasoned with real-life examples of these

---

[2] As Greg Flood of Ironshore says, "Most of my scar tissue over the years is from the unexpected happening on the best-underwritten accounts."

principles in action. It's my sincere hope that this book, at least in some small way, will help you do your job better and/or gain a greater understanding of D&O Insurance. It'll be a bonus if you get a few chuckles as well.

One more blanket disclaimer: I'd like to emphasize that the concepts discussed in this book are of a general and theoretical nature and certainly many exceptions apply to what's laid out herein. As always, the actual terms and conditions of a specific policy in question (as well as other particular facts) will govern the coverage provided under an insurance policy. Further, I am not dispensing any legal, accounting or tax advice in this book and nothing written herein should be relied upon as such; please consult a qualified professional when seeking such insights.

Thanks once again for buying this book, I hope you enjoy it – to the greatest extent that an insurance book can be enjoyed, that is!

The 30,000 Foot View of D&O Insurance

I've participated in hundreds, possibly thousands, of underwriting and claims meetings during my professional lines insurance (henceforth simply "professional lines") career. You realize during the course of listening to so many people speak that certain buzzwords and catchphrases go in and out of fashion. One enduring phrase, however, is "the 30,000-foot view." This is, obviously, a big-picture overview of an issue, which can then be augmented by "drilling down into" or "getting granular about" more particulars. So here's your 30,000-foot view of D&O Insurance. We'll drill down into the granularity of it later.

Someone pointed out to me early in my career that D&O Insurance stands out in the world of commercial insurance because it involves the insuring of people's behavior, always a risky thing. A million-dollar warehouse may burn to the ground, but you can be sure that it won't embezzle $50 billion from anyone. Or harass them. Or defame them. And it's not always easy to put a monetary figure on those types of losses, whereas the loss of a million dollars' worth of warehouse structure and contents is a bit easier to assess.

Because you're dealing with human beings and their behavior, right off the bat one could argue that there's an element of psychology involved. How is this person going to react when they're under pressure? Will they seek competent outside advice or are they so confident (and/or egotistical) that they'll attempt to go it alone? Do they appear to be a straight shooter who always follows the guidelines and complies with company policy and external laws or will they cut corners to achieve their objective at all costs?

You can't pick up on most of these intangible factors from reviewing one-dimensional insurance applications, but sometimes they come to the fore when meeting an applicant in person.

One of my favorite stories in this regard involves a bank D&O account that we quoted when I was at AIG. The underwriting manager went to a meeting with the bank's entire board of directors. They met in the bank's headquarters boardroom. This is not as common today, but it occurred more frequently back in a hard market when D&O Insurance was more difficult to obtain, and insureds took even more of a personal interest in the product.

The CEO was the last one to arrive. When he walked into the room, the CFO said, "Frank, I've saved a seat for you here at the head of the table."

The CEO replied: "Anywhere I sit is the head of the table."

Our underwriter said he was so annoyed by the CEO's arrogance that he wanted to add $10,000 to the quote (but I don't believe he did; just want to make that clear for any insurance regulators who might read this).

When it comes to assessing people's personalities and behaviors, I've developed a number of theories over the years. One rather pedestrian example involves company lapel pins. It's not nearly as prevalent on either coast of the United States, but in the Midwest certain companies are chock full of employees who take great pride in working for their employer. This seems especially true when that employer is one of the largest and most respected businesses in that particular town or state. Visit these companies and you'll notice that a majority of the workers are wearing the employer's logo pin on the lapel of their suit. I know it sounds inane, but I find that these companies have a more engaged, enthusiastic and diligent workforce. I won't go so far as to say that I've ever done a study to prove my theory, but I'd bet that lapel-pin-wearing workforces have a lower incidence of employment-related lawsuits and overall higher productivity.

I'll try to respect your time by not wasting it with too many tangents, but I can't mention lapel pins without recounting my absolute favorite lapel-pin story. It was told to me by a good friend at insurance broking giant Willis.

Joseph Plumeri, the CEO of Willis (who did a remarkable job after taking over in 2000 and before stepping down in 2013), was a strong advocate of employees wearing lapel pins. I assume he believed it's a tangible symbol of company pride and passion, although I can't say for sure. Anyway, it was well known in the halls of Willis that employees were encouraged to wear Willis lapel pins daily. If an employee happened to run into Mr. Plumeri while not wearing one, it could be a bit awkward.

One morning a Willis broker, lacking a lapel pin that day, rushed into the main reception area at the company's New York headquarters and found himself staring straight at Mr. Plumeri.

"Where is your lapel pin?" Mr. Plumeri supposedly asked.

What happened next, which I'm told is 100 percent true, is now legendary at Willis. The broker, upon looking down and realizing there was no Willis lapel pin affixed to his suit coat, said to Mr. Plumeri in a shocked tone: "Damn, I must've left it on my pajamas!"

Mr. Plumeri reportedly laughed.

Moving beyond lapel pins, there are a wide variety of intangibles that may be considered on any particular D&O account. I'm not saying they're all relevant in every instance; indeed, most times, especially when dealing with a high volume of smaller accounts, no consideration of intangibles is necessary at all. Nonetheless, in my view, "holistic underwriting" (another buzzword that has seen its popularity rise and fall), which takes into account a variety of factors, not all of which show up on the standard underwriting worksheet, is an important concept. I believe that this is especially beneficial on larger accounts, generally those falling in the Fortune 1000 range or thereabouts.

While we're up here at 30,000 feet, it might be helpful to point out for some readers a basic distinction between D&O,

or "management liability," and Errors & Omissions ("E&O") insurance, also known as "professional liability" or, in England and other places outside America, "professional indemnity." For our purposes in this book, the terms D&O and management liability will be used interchangeably, as will E&O and professional liability, with apologies to our English friends for not using "professional indemnity." The term "executive liability" is also used interchangeably with D&O at some companies, but we'll skip that one altogether.

The main function of D&O Insurance, historically, was to protect a company's directors and officers against claims arising from a variety of sources. But, in reality, the majority of claim dollars were paid to resolve public company shareholder class actions. Over the years, as the D&O market has softened (i.e. become more favorable for insureds because of competition among carriers due to generally favorable loss experiences), D&O policies have been broadened to respond to claims from regulators (both domestic and foreign), employees, job applicants and others. Of course, this coverage has expanded and contracted as the market has changed.

By contrast, the main function of E&O insurance is, generally, to protect a company and its employees from claims brought by customers or clients.

I'm sure most people reading this book already knew that distinction, but experience has taught me that sometimes it doesn't hurt to state the obvious. This calls to mind a story from when I was at AIG. I instructed a new underwriter with no professional lines experience (we had just hired him from a life insurance company) to obtain some facultative reinsurance[3], frequently referred to simply as "fac" in the industry, for a particular account. He agreed to do so and left my office with the appearance that he knew what he was doing. Later that day I passed him in the hallway, and he said to me, "Larry, I'm working on getting that *dac* for you."

I asked him to repeat what he had just said, and he did.

"You don't know what fac is, do you?" I asked.

He sheepishly admitted he didn't and that he intended to have another underwriter help him with the task later in the day. This is one of the examples that lead me to err on the side of explaining the obvious. Too many people follow the adage "You can remain silent and allow people to assume you're ignorant, or you can open your mouth and prove it."

I've demonstrated time and again that I don't adhere to that philosophy!

***

---

[3] Facultative reinsurance normally applies to a single specific risk. For example, if a carrier is not comfortable writing a full $25 million limit of liability on a particular D&O account, it might seek to have a reinsurer assume the top $10 million layer of that limit (expressed as $10mm x/s of $15mm p/o $25mm in insurance shorthand). This would be facultative reinsurance. On the other hand, "treaty" reinsurance generally applies to an entire book of business automatically. For example, a reinsurer may agree to reinsure the $5 million layer of liability in excess of the first $5 million layer of liability across the board on all $10 million D&O policies that a carrier writes on a particular class of business, such as private companies with sales of less than $50 million annually.

I've read a supposedly authoritative history that said the first D&O Insurance policy in the United States was written in 1962 by St. Paul. Another source, cited by the learned and legendary former Marsh broker Bill Brown, states that the first D&O policies for U.S. companies were written in the 1930s by Lloyd's in response to the American stock market crash and the passage of the two major U.S. securities acts (Bill wasn't actually around yet to see those policies bound). This account even names the first two insureds: Federated Department Stores and Flintkote Company[4]. (The actual policies have just recently been issued in both cases... Just kidding, policy issuance can take a long time with some carriers, but it's not quite that bad!)

While I can't say with certainty who wrote (or purchased) the first D&O Insurance policy, I can provide an explanation of the origins of the term "underwriter," a decidedly British creation spawned at Lloyd's.

The Lloyd's insurance market evolved from gatherings of men at Edward Lloyd's coffee house on Tower Street in London in 1688. In those days, coffee shops were frequented by the moneyed class (also true today for those who can afford Starbucks). These wealthy individuals sipping java at Lloyd's were solicited to provide insurance for cargo ships. Shipping was much more perilous in those days than today because of rudimentary navigation equipment and less advanced ship

---

[4] A former manufacturer of building materials, Flintkote ceased operations in the 1980s and declared bankruptcy in 2004 due to heavy losses stemming from more than 350,000 asbestos claims.

construction. Each voyage carried a significant possibility of sinking.

Ship owners seeking insurance for a particular voyage would hire a "broker" to arrange for the insurance. The broker would write the ship's name on a sheet of paper, along with the particulars of the journey (e.g. expected route and ports of call). He would also set forth the value of the ship itself and of its cargo, as well as the terms of the requested insurance deal – the amount of premium that the owner was offering and the specific limit of liability he desired. The broker would then make the rounds among the wealthy Lloyd's patrons, soliciting them to take a portion of the risk. Investors who wanted to participate would write their name under the ship's name and the rest of the assorted particulars of the deal to show that they intended to be bound for a certain percentage of the overall limit of liability. Thus, they became known as "underwriters" and they were said to be "underwriting" risk. This was the origin of modern marine insurance.

By the way, the London insurance market took the name "Lloyd's" not only because Edward Lloyd's coffee shop was the site of all of these dealings,[5] but also because, upon watching these insurance arrangements being consummated in his establishment, Mr. Lloyd started documenting the specifics of each deal to help everyone keep track of their various obligations. Like any good businessman, he charged a

---

[5] In 1771 a group of 79 underwriters left Lloyd's coffee shop and established an insurance exchange in a nearby building, but they maintained the Lloyd's name.

fee for his services. Thus, Edward Lloyd functioned as the first back office of the insurance industry. (There's no record on his performance with policy issuance.)

One of the broker's chief responsibilities during this process was to ensure that he was only signing people who had the financial wherewithal to make their payment should the need arise. These investors were known as "names" – a word still used today to identify Lloyd's backers. Whereas today companies are allowed to underwrite risk at Lloyd's, in the old days only individuals were eligible to do so. And, paradoxically, the people known as "names" were actually identified by numbers, not their actual names. Those crazy Brits strike again.

In the early days of D&O in America, primarily in the late 1960s/early 1970s, there were three main carriers: Lloyd's, AIG and CNA (whose program was managed by Stewart Smith). Don Fischer, an esteemed industry veteran (recently retired) who worked in the trenches of AIG, believes that most insureds probably didn't know what went on behind the scenes: "Lloyd's reinsured AIG for a significant portion of each risk and they were the major reinsurer of CNA as well, so, really, it was like there was just one market. When we wanted to quote something at AIG, we'd have to send a telex, or cable as it was also known, to Lloyd's and await their permission. They'd write back 'Clear to quote DANDO.' They didn't use an ampersand; it was just 'DANDO.' They also would opine on our suggested price, and we usually agreed with their final premium. After all, we had no other competition!"

Don remembers a gentleman coming to AIG's New York offices in those early days seeking D&O Insurance coverage for his chain of hamburger joints. He told everyone who'd listen at AIG that his company was going to be big and that he needed D&O Insurance to protect it. Don says the man received a skeptical response. He remembers this particular fellow because he would later run across his name again.

It was Ray Kroc, and his company was McDonald's.

Don was also present for the filing of one of the first major claims in U.S. D&O history by a large Long Island utility. "Nobody really knew how to handle a D&O claim because there hadn't really been any, so Hank Greenberg hired George D'Amato to represent AIG. That claim really got AIG's attention and, from what I remember, for a while the company actually thought about exiting the line of business."

***

A factor that makes working in D&O Insurance interesting and engaging is that senior executives of a company usually take a great interest in the D&O Insurance because it protects the executives' personal wealth and, in some cases, their reputations. The general counsel of a company has no personal stake in ensuring that adequate fire insurance is in place for a warehouse in Tacoma, but he wants to make sure that there's plenty of D&O Insurance coverage to prevent a shareholder suit from gobbling up his life savings and forcing him to sell his beach house.

Thus, senior executives are more likely to meet with D&O underwriters when requested to give them more of a "peek under the hood" than underwriters in other lines of insurance would get. D&O Insurance underwriters also get treated to rounds of golf, tickets to sporting events, nice meals and a whole host of other enjoyable experiences that are just "part of the job." During one stretch when I was playing a particularly significant amount of golf for work in a short period, one of my colleagues said to me "If you joined the PGA Tour, you'd probably play less golf than you're playing right now."

Hey, somebody had to do it.

In the pages that follow, I'm going to provide some insights into the D&O Insurance underwriting process, highlighting some factors I think are particularly relevant. What I'd emphasize, however, is that no instructional manual or underwriting worksheet can serve as a "one size fits all" solution for all D&O accounts. Rather, I attempt to open your mind to consideration of various factors that should be weighed in the underwriting process while also encouraging you to think about underwriting rationally and, possibly, to develop your own formula for assessing each unique risk on its own merits. As I was famous for repeating often while training underwriters at AIG and ACE: *"There's a rational basis for everything we do."* Sometimes that rational basis is quite clear and concrete, while other times it is divined from less obvious (a.k.a. "soft") factors.

The four squares of a D&O underwriting worksheet or pricing formula should be a starting point, but certainly not a static solution that's mindlessly applied to every account. There's a lot of merit to the old saying "To a man with a hammer, every problem looks like a nail." To a man with a D&O Insurance underwriting worksheet, every account should not necessarily look like it can be fully and accurately assessed. I know, my version of that saying, adapted for underwriting purposes, is not as catchy as the original.

I hope that at least some of what you read on the following pages provides you with a deeper insight into D&O Insurance and helps you do your job better in some way.

Underwriting D&O Insurance

Directors and Officers Liability Insurance is, undeniably, the most prominent of professional lines insurance products. D&O Insurance is the product most frequently cited, according to my informal observations, when a professional lines insurance practitioner is trying to explain his job to a non-insurance person.

Stranger at cocktail party: "So, what do you do?"
Professional Lines Underwriter: "I'm involved in professional lines insurance underwriting."
Stranger: "What's that, like my car or homeowner's insurance?"
Underwriter: "No, Directors and Officers Liability Insurance, D&O. It protects boards of directors."
Stranger: "Oh, yeah, I think my father-in-law buys that for his company." [Quickly returns the conversation to the Giants' Super Bowl chances.]

There are a number of factors underlying the allure of D&O Insurance to professional lines people. One is its relatively high premium rates compared to other professional lines products. A valuable piece of career advice that I've been imparting to young underwriters for years – but which has almost universally fallen on deaf ears – is that they would be wise to focus on learning how to underwrite fidelity bonds, a product whose experts within the industry are generally older and beginning to retire. There's a serious need for young fidelity bond underwriting talent, but because the rate-per-million on bonds is generally lower than D&O and the product isn't viewed as being as "sexy," most young underwriters don't want to touch it with a 10-foot *pro rata* wheel. Maybe a self-confident 20-something reading this book will see the wisdom in my advice and make me proud!

Another driver of D&O's popularity as a career choice is the fact that it's so important to people at the highest levels of insured companies. If you're an underwriter, discussing the boiler and machinery coverage is not nearly as likely to get you an audience with an insured's CEO and other senior executives as is talking about the D&O program. People like to be associated with the high-profile, high-revenue products; it's not a big mystery.

A. Getting Started

As discussed earlier, D&O Insurance's primary purpose is to protect the personal assets of a company's directors and officers. That's why boards of directors are so concerned about getting adequate (or better) coverage and why it looms so prominently on the radar of almost every publicly-traded company.

When an underwriter approached me during my days as a senior underwriting manager with a request to customize an insured's D&O policy, I would remind them that we would only cover *insurable* risks and that certain exposures were uninsurable and simply a part of the cost of doing business. These risks weren't within the universe of what we'd cover. Making the distinction between these two classes of risk, of course, is the key to adhering to that philosophy.

The litmus test that I use to identify an insurable risk is to determine whether that risk can be logically assessed (or "*underwritten to*," as we say in the business) and, if so, whether it properly falls within the ambit of a D&O policy.

For example, just about every D&O policy on the market contains an exclusion for loss arising from personal injury or bodily damage. If a broker were to ask to have that exclusion removed because his client had two particularly combative officers who were given to losing their tempers and striking employees at any time, I would refuse the request. First, you can't logically predict what might upset an individual to the point where they'll express their anger physically. It could be a fight with a spouse that morning, failure to take prescribed medication, a traffic accident on the way to work or any of a number of fateful events. But more important, covering personal injuries incurred by an individual in an altercation is simply not within the traditional contemplation of a D&O policy, which addresses the risks in the normal course of *managing* a business. Physically hitting employees is not a normal occurrence in running a company. Plus, health insurance should be available to respond to such incidents, at least for the medical costs, and the liability portion could be covered elsewhere, such as by a comprehensive general liability ("CGL") policy and/or personal umbrella policy (as always, check your specific policy for applicable wording!)

A classic example of a risk that is not insurable under a D&O policy comes to mind from my days of practicing law at D'Amato & Lynch. Our client had written D&O coverage for a company in the Midwest that had accepted delivery of a new truck. For some reason, the company refused to pay the truck dealer's bill. The company got sued and it turned to our client, the insurer, for payment of the outstanding bill. The insured company contended that the cost of the truck was "Loss" arising from a "Claim" under its D&O policy.

Our client's contention was that there was no "Loss" (as defined under the policy) because the company had received a brand-new truck of some value and any amounts that the company ultimately had to pay to the truck dealer would simply be compensation for a value received. Thus, there was no net loss. Eventually, this insured saw the wisdom of our client's position and withdrew its claim. Paying for goods received is not within the scope of a D&O policy's proper operation.

This same reasoning is at work when a carrier declines to cover so-called "bump up" claims under a D&O policy. A bump-up claim can arise when a company makes a tender offer to buy the shares of another company, usually in a takeover situation. Many times, the shareholders of the target company will sue, saying that the acquirer didn't pay enough for their shares. Let's say the original deal was struck at $100 per share, but a court later rules that a fair and appropriate price would have been $125 per share. The court then orders the acquirer to pay another $25 per share to the target company's former shareholders. If the acquirer files a claim under its D&O policy seeking coverage for the payment of that $25 differential, most D&O carriers would deny the claim on the grounds that the acquirer actually bought stock worth $125 per share (according to the court's decision), thus it suffered no "loss" under the policy since the additional $25 per share merely represented adequate payment for value received.

Having said the above, many D&O carriers in today's market have broadened their coverage for bump-up claims to provide defense costs and payment of amounts which directors and officers owe that are non-indemnifiable. However, generally insurers still would not cover the cost of increasing the tender offer amount. I say "generally" because you never know what a particular carrier will offer to cover in a particular situation, especially in a soft market when carriers are anxious to get premium on the books.

As the old saying goes, almost everything in life is negotiable.

Now that we have a basic understanding of what D&O Insurance is intended to cover, let's take a closer look at how the typical policy works.

B. Breaking down the D&O Policy

A typical D&O policy has a lot of moving parts, all serving a specific purpose and precisely interacting with one or more other sections of the policy to create the overall coverage package. As seasoned insurance professionals know – as well as lawyers and business people in general, for that matter – every word and punctuation mark matters. There have been multi-million-dollar lawsuits fought over the meaning of the placement (or omission) of a single punctuation mark.

D&O Insurance policies continue to evolve over time in step with changes in the business, legal and regulatory environment of the United States and, more recently, overseas as well. The D&O policy truly is becoming global in nature.

I could drill down into every last bit of minutiae of the typical D&O Insurance policy, but that would be tedious and probably not worth your time. Instead, I will examine the major sections of the standard policy and focus on specific points of particular interest for underwriters, brokers and insureds.

You'll note that in many instances terms that would normally be capitalized, and possibly set in bold face in a standard D&O policy, are presented in lower case here. That's because unless specifically stated, those terms aren't used in reference to any particular policy's definition, but rather in a generic manner.

It's important to point out that almost all D&O Insurance policies on the market today (I avoid absolute statements like "all D&O policies" because the D&O market is large and constantly changing) are written on a "claims made and reported" basis. This is in contrast to policies written on an "occurrence" basis, such as the typical medical malpractice insurance policy and most CGL insurance policies.

The difference is this: In order to be eligible for coverage under a claims made and reported D&O Insurance policy, a claim must be first made against one or more insureds and reported to the carrier during the policy period (or extended reporting period, if applicable). That traditional requirement, however, has been softened over the years as the market has become more competitive. Nowadays, many carriers standardly allow for an extended window of 60 or 90 days after a D&O policy period's expiration to report a claim. However, some insurers who allow this extra reporting period stipulate that it only applies to claims first made within the specified number of extended days granted. So, for example, a carrier may say the insured has an extra 60 days from the policy's expiration to report a claim provided it is reported within 60 days of that claim first being made. This means the insured would only ever get the full 60-day reporting extension if the claim was first made on the last day of the policy period. Some policies also restrict this additional reporting window to only lawsuits and not other types of claims or notices of potential claims. Again, and as is true for statements made throughout this book, the actual terms and conditions of a specific policy must be consulted to determine how the coverage works.

Occurrence policies, on the other hand, provide coverage for claims arising from "occurrences" (as defined in the policy) that take place during the policy period – no matter when the resulting claim comes to fruition. So, for example, if a surgeon left a scalpel in a patient's stomach in 2005 but the patient didn't discover the error and file a lawsuit until 2010, a typical medical malpractice occurrence policy would respond to the claim. Generally, as long as the "occurrence" happens while the occurrence policy is in effect, there's no limitation on when the claim can be brought, other than, of course, any applicable legal statute of limitations governing that particular type of claim. In some jurisdictions the statute of limitations will start running when the occurrence takes place and in others it begins only after the wrongful act is first discovered by the aggrieved party. And some jurisdictions use a combination of both (e.g. six years after the act occurred or three years after it was first discovered by the plaintiff.)

1. The Insuring Agreements

Insuring agreements are the heart of a D&O policy. They establish in general terms what, and who, will receive coverage. In a sense, they're the seeds from which all other parts of the policy grow.

Up until the 1990s, most D&O policies had two insuring agreements, almost uniformly designated as Insuring Agreement A and Insuring Agreement B. (Insurers are lemming-like in many ways and don't mind copying each other to a fair degree.) These two sections of the policy were also known, colloquially, as the "A Side" and the "B Side." The A Side insured the directors and officers individually when they were not indemnified by the insured company for a claim against them because the insured company either didn't have the funds or was prohibited by law or its by-laws from providing indemnification.

The B Side of the policy provided coverage in the form of reimbursement to the insured company after it paid the losses of its directors and officers for a covered claim. Almost all D&O policies have been, for as long as anyone can remember, structured as "reimbursement" policies, meaning the carrier has no duty to provide a defense to its insureds, but rather it reimburses them after they've paid losses, including defense costs. This alleviates the need for the insurer to choose defense counsel and, theoretically, make other decisions which could result in liability to the carrier if things should go wrong.

Given that many D&O claims are complex matters involving high stakes, sometimes even determining whether a defendant company will survive as an ongoing entity, carriers tend to prefer to have a say in what happens – but they don't want to be seen as having too much control in the proceedings, something which most insureds wouldn't like anyway. For example, insurers generally reserve the right to approve the insured's choice of defense counsel in a D&O claim. At least one major carrier has even established a list of pre-approved "panel counsel" law firms from which insureds must choose their defense counsel for securities class action claims. Only on rare occasions will this insurer make a special exception and allow a law firm not on the pre-approved list to defend a securities class action claim at the insured's request.

Generally, there is no self-insured retention (also called an "SIR" or, simply, a "retention") for losses covered under the A Side (non-indemnifiable) insuring agreement, although there are some rare exceptions to this rule not worth discussing here. The reason for this, obviously, is that if individual directors and officers (not coincidentally, the people who usually decide which policy to buy) are forced to defend a claim without the benefit of reimbursement from the insured company, it would create quite a financial burden for them to personally satisfy a large SIR.

Usually, a relatively significant self-insured retention applies to claims covered under the B Side of the D&O policy. For example, for a company carrying a $5 million limit of liability, it wouldn't be unusual to have a $250,000 or even $500,000 SIR on the policy for indemnifiable loss. Sometimes an even larger SIR may apply. But remember: As a general rule, there are exceptions to every general rule in professional lines insurance.

A word here about the difference between an SIR and a "deductible," the latter being a term that most people are familiar with from their homeowners or auto insurance. As with many terms in the insurance industry, the exact definitions and usage may vary from carrier to carrier; always consult the specific wording of a policy in question for a reliable answer. However, generally, an SIR represents covered loss that an insured must pay out of pocket before the insurer will start paying covered loss in excess of that amount. The insured is said to have to "satisfy the retention" before the carrier will start writing checks. So, for example, if an insured has a $1 million limit of liability (also known in shorthand as the "limit") on its D&O policy with a $100,000 retention, the insured will have to pay $100,000 of covered loss out of its own pocket before the carrier will start paying some or all of its $1 million limit.

A deductible, by contrast, normally reduces the policy's total limit of liability, unlike an SIR. So, for example, if you had a $1 million homeowners' insurance policy with a $10,000 deductible, the carrier would only be liable to pay up to $990,000 in total losses. You'd be on the hook for the first $10,000 of covered loss. Also, again depending upon the specific way that "deductible" is defined in a policy, a carrier may pay the entire claim amount to a third party (assuming it's a liability claim) and then pursue the insured for reimbursement of the deductible amount separately.

In 1995 a new insuring agreement was introduced into D&O policies. This Insuring Agreement C (or C-Side Coverage) protected a corporate entity for its own liability (apart from the liability of individual directors and officers) arising from claims involving allegations of wrongdoing in connection with the company's securities. This was purportedly done to avoid disputes between carriers and insureds over allocating loss between what was attributable to directors and officers (covered) and what was attributable to the corporate entity (not previously covered.)

Some carriers charged an additional premium for this expanded coverage, a nice benefit for their bottom line in the relatively soft market of the mid- and late-1990s, while others provided it at no additional cost with the thought that the certainty created by addressing the allocation issue up front saved time and money in resolving coverage disputes down the road. The new C-Side coverage quickly caught on, despite there being a school of thought that carriers were selling an illusory enhancement. In at least some jurisdictions it appeared that the insurer would be on the hook for the entire claim when individual directors and officers were named as defendants in conjunction with the corporate entity in a securities lawsuit. Nonetheless, insureds seemed to prefer the certainty of having the corporate securities coverage built right into their policy form rather than hoping that their claim, if they did get one, would arise in a jurisdiction predisposed toward finding full coverage when both individuals and the corporate entity were named as defendants. Not having this fairly-low cost (or free) enhancement seemed to be a gamble that the typical risk manager didn't want to take, especially when contemplating the prospect of having to explain this available feature's absence to a board of directors after a securities claim was filed.

Today there are even more insuring agreements available on a D&O policy. And there may well be others created between the time this paragraph is written and you actually read it. Among the additional insuring agreements currently available are those that cover:

Individual insureds when serving on outside boards (usually at the direction or request of the policy's insured entity and sometimes the request to serve must be in writing in order for the individual to be covered);

Public relations costs to address a crisis that may adversely affect an insured company's reputation and/or stock price;

Costs arising from an investigation into the allegations made by one or more company shareholders presenting a derivative demand on the board of directors; and

Costs arising from regulatory and/or criminal investigations, including those taking place in foreign (i.e. non-U.S.) jurisdictions.

Other insuring agreements can be added by endorsement, of course, but the key is to ensure that a D&O policy's insuring agreements create coverage that's appropriate for the insured's needs. This is largely the broker's obligation, not the underwriter's, although it's imperative that an underwriter fully understand the operations of the insured, regardless of whether they're all covered or not.

And again, remember that virtually all D&O policies today are "claims made and reported" policies, meaning that the claim must first be made against one or more insureds and reported to the insurer during the policy period. Over the years, there have been "occurrence" D&O policies introduced into the market, but they have generally not been offered for long. Making actuarial judgments is difficult enough with a claims made and reported D&O policy that has a definite expiration date for the reporting of claims (some claims can drag out for 6 years or more before resolution); adding the longer reporting period (or "tail") of an occurrence policy makes a tough task exponentially more difficult.

2. The Definitions

The Definitions section of a D&O policy, as many insureds have come to learn after it's too late, contains a lot of restrictive language and shapes the overall scope of coverage significantly. In many instances, the definitions become supplemental exclusions – especially the definition of Loss, as you'll see below. The meaning of significant terms should never be overlooked or taken lightly in any contract, but this is particularly true with an insurance policy, which, after all, is simply a type of contract.

While each definition in a D&O Insurance policy is important, I'm not going to review every single defined term that you'd find in a survey of all the D&O policies on today's market. That would easily fill a book by itself (and you thought THIS book was boring!). However, I will examine most of the major defined terms. As you'd imagine, there isn't absolute uniformity among D&O policies when it comes to defined terms – or anything else, really – so I'm examining generic versions of most definitions.

I should note that many of these terms are defined in the same or a similar manner in some other types of professional lines insurance policies as well, so the analysis below may help in other areas.

Application

The definition of the Application is critical because it establishes which materials and information the carrier is relying upon in underwriting the D&O policy. And that's significant because if there are misrepresentations, either intentional or inadvertent, in those materials, the carrier may claim that it was misled in the underwriting process and therefore a valid contract evidencing mutual agreement was not issued. This can be the basis for a complete rescission of the insurance policy or, possibly, just a denial of a specific claim, depending upon the facts involved.

For example, let's assume that an applicant company admits, after a claim is filed against it for financial mismanagement, that it misstated its yearly revenues by 75 percent in its annual report, which was deemed to be a part of the Application. The carrier may contend that had it known the true revenue figures during the underwriting process, it would never have agreed to bind the policy in question. Or maybe it will take the position that it wouldn't have bound the policy with the particular limit of liability, retention and/or premium that it did. Or, possibly, it would've included additional exclusions and other restrictions on the policy that would've applied to the recent claim.

What's essential from the applicant's and broker's perspective is that they understand exactly what information the carrier is relying upon in underwriting the policy and that all such information is *accurate*. These days, in a relatively "soft" insurance market (which works in the insureds' favor), applicants are generally successful in getting the definition of the Application restricted to only information released in the previous year. In certain circumstances, however, carriers may declare that the previous three- or five-years' worth of information shall be considered part of the Application.

Another enhancement that an insured can request is that the Application be deemed to only consist of materials that were *actually reviewed* during the underwriting process. Is it fair for a carrier, after a costly claim is filed, to go back and "re-underwrite" the policy in order to find a discrepancy in the Application that wasn't caught – and wasn't relied upon – the first time around? If the underwriter never relied upon the unfavorable facts during the original underwriting process, many would argue that it's unfair for the carrier to now use those facts as a basis for rescission of the entire policy – or even just as a basis for excluding a particular claim. To establish this limited reliance on specific materials, an applicant company can present the carrier with the list of materials to be reviewed during the underwriting process as part of the Application and request a letter of intent (or, better, an endorsement to the policy) stating that the carrier only relied upon those materials in underwriting the policy.

A key concept to understand with respect to the Application (and which is also relevant to the Exclusions section, but I will discuss that below) is that of "severability." When a carrier grants severability of the Application, it means that the representations contained therein are deemed severed, or made separately, as among the individual insureds and the corporate entity. So, with severability, if the CEO deliberately makes a misrepresentation on the Application, normally the individual director and officer insureds won't be denied their insurance coverage under the A Side of the policy. The other "innocent" insureds are deemed to be "severed" from liability for the CEO's misrepresentations. However, pursuant to a provision that is frequently included in D&O policies, if those individual directors and officers knew the truth about the misrepresented information, they too may be denied coverage under the A Side. Some policies state that just knowing the truth is enough to negate coverage for the individuals, while other policies require that they not only knew the truth about the misrepresentation but that they also knew it was being misrepresented to the insurance carrier as part of the Application.

Again, every policy and Application are different (a common theme throughout this book; just consider it to be repeated herein constantly even though I refrain from doing so explicitly to minimize the snooze factor!) and must be consulted individually.

Another aspect to severability of the Application is that the misrepresentations of specified individuals will many times be attributed to the corporate entity itself, thereby withholding reimbursement coverage under the policy's B Side if these people make a false representation. These designated individuals are usually the CEO, the CFO and the general counsel (sometimes known as the "C-Suite") as well as, sometimes, the risk manager and the person who actually signed the application. And sometimes it can be some combination of the aforementioned. Severability is an important feature to have on a D&O policy from an insured's viewpoint since it protects innocent insureds from the loss of coverage due to the misrepresentations of one or more of their colleagues.

Claim

Like many other provisions in the typical D&O policy, the definition of a "Claim" has broadened over the years as the market has softened and competition among carriers has increased. In earlier years, the definition of a Claim was restricted to merely a written demand for money damages made upon an insured during the policy period. This could come in the form of an actual lawsuit, or simply a demand letter or other written communication. Periodically, insureds and brokers would ask underwriters to broaden this definition to include verbal demands for money, but underwriters would usually resist, saying that the claims analyst would need a written document in order to properly review and adjust the Claim. And while that sounded on its face like a bit of a weak rationalization, there was quite a bit of logic to it. Adjusting a claim based upon "he said/she said" accounts of a conversation is not easy.

Eventually, the definition of Claim broadened to include such things as requests for non-monetary damages (e.g. injunctive relief) and investigative inquiries of individual insureds and/or the insured company. The specifics of the definition's liberalization depended, of course, upon the particular carrier and policy involved. And also, some would joke, the time of the month that the request was made. It has long been an industry saying, accurate or not, that certain carriers are considerably more liberal in their underwriting standards at the end of the month when they're desperate for more premium dollars to reach their monthly or quarterly financial goals.

Many insureds seek to broaden the definition of Claim, instinctively thinking that "broader is better." This is not always the case, however. One must remember that there is a _duty_ to report a claim under the D&O policy, usually within specified time parameters. So, for example, if the definition of Claim is expanded to include oral demands, which some carriers are doing in today's market, it creates a much more difficult burden of notification. The insured entity is now required to report every oral demand made against any insured. A lawsuit filed against the insureds in the current policy period may turn out to be the manifestation of an oral demand that was made on the insured's general counsel two years ago but was never reported to the carrier. Thus, that particular lawsuit most likely would not qualify as a Claim since it wasn't first made in the current policy period.

As was discussed previously, the timing of reporting a Claim is critical under any D&O policy. Many of today's forms require that the claim be reported "*as soon as practicable*" and then go on to say, "*but in no event later than 60 days from the date that the Claim was first made.*" Or they may say "*but in no event later than the expiration of the policy period."* In recent years, due to softening market conditions, many carriers have expanded this provision to automatically include an additional 60 or 90 days to report the Claim after the policy's expiration. Some carriers have restricted that enhancement, however, to an additional 60 or 90 days as long as the Claim is still reported within 60 or 90 days of first being made, thus, the insured would only get the full extension period granted if the Claim was first made on the very last day of the policy period. Note: I've set forth this reporting information twice now only because it is so critical to the operation of a D&O Insurance policy and should not be taken lightly.

Defense Costs

Coverage for defense costs is a vital component of any D&O policy. Defense costs can constitute a considerable portion of a claim's total costs – or even the entire amount if the claim is successfully defended. Virtually every carrier uses the same language in declaring that only "reasonable and necessary" fees, costs, charges and expenses are covered. How one defines "reasonable and necessary" is, of course, of pivotal importance. Some carriers use what they call "Litigation Guidelines" to govern the interpretation of "reasonable and necessary." For instance, these guidelines may dictate that a law firm can only charge a maximum of 10 cents per page for photocopies and may not bill for the attendance of more than one lawyer at depositions. While it's obviously in the best interests of both the insureds and the carrier to preserve as much of a policy's limits as possible, the insureds also don't want to be tethered to unreasonably thrifty litigation guidelines that hamper a law firm's effectiveness. Litigation guidelines can certainly serve an important purpose if they are drafted appropriately and are updated regularly to keep pace with an ever-changing business and legal environment. A prudent and worthwhile exercise for any insured considering the purchase of D&O coverage would be to obtain any prospective carrier's litigation guidelines (assuming they use them, not all do) to ensure that they are acceptable before binding coverage. Also, it would behoove the applicant company to make sure in advance of any claim that the outside law firm(s) it intends to use would be acceptable to the D&O carrier. I've seen many instances of bitter feuding between an insured and a D&O carrier over the use of a particular law firm that the insured wanted to use but the carrier found objectionable. This is an issue that should be addressed before binding the D&O policy if at all possible.

Some in the insurance industry, especially insureds and defense lawyers, may think that carriers unnecessarily "crack the whip" when it comes to reviewing and paying defense costs under a D&O policy. But that's not always true. A carrier's careful review of defense-cost bills and suggestions on defense strategies can yield significant savings, thus preserving a policy's limits for other uses, such as payment of settlements or for use in future claims under the same policy year. Some carriers employ legal audit firms to review all defense bills, while others use their outside coverage counsel or in-house claims analysts for this purpose.

When I was working for the legendary Bill Cotter at Parker, Coulter, Daley & White in Boston in the early 1990s, Bill was acting as coverage counsel for a carrier on a major claim in Colorado. The case's settlement conference adjourned on a Friday and was to be continued the following Monday. Bill decided to stay in Colorado for the weekend to ski at one of the state's renowned slopes. Bill was in the ski-lift line when he bumped into one of the defense lawyers who said he'd like to discuss the case with Bill in the restaurant on top of the mountain. Months later, when that lawyer's invoice came to Bill for review, he noticed a $50 charge for "transportation costs to conference with coverage counsel." The attorney had tried to bill the carrier for his ski-lift ticket to the restaurant on top of the mountain! Bill, needless to say, weeded out that charge. In another case, a lawyer who had forgotten his dress shoes on a business trip purchased new shoes in his destination city and tried to pawn off the cost on the carrier. But Bill disallowed the charge after further inquiry. It had been submitted as "ground transportation costs." These are only minor examples, but unjustified costs like these can add up to big dollars over the course of a lawsuit. And, of course, there are many other examples that aren't so minor.

Employment Practices Wrongful Act

Many D&O policies today offer coverage for claims arising from employment practices, something that was specifically excluded in earlier times. As the market has softened, the employment practices coverage available in a D&O policy has concurrently broadened. Now, employment practices liability (EPL) coverage can be obtained through a D&O policy for a wide array of employment practices wrongful acts, including retaliation, bullying, wrongful failure to hire or promote someone, employment-related misrepresentation to an employee or applicant, negligent evaluation of employees, failure to grant tenure, employment-related slander, libel, humiliation or defamation and wrongful discipline. The complete list is longer than that and, no doubt, will continue to expand. Loss arising from almost any employment-related wrongful act that you can think of can be covered, even loss arising from workplace violence, although that coverage usually comes in a separate policy.

On the face of it, from an insured's perspective, this expansion of a D&O policy into EPL coverage would seem beneficial, but that's not always the case. When a director or senior officer of an insured is told that her D&O limits might be impaired – or even totally exhausted – by the employment practices violations of a colleague in a far-flung field office, they usually aren't happy. Prudent risk-management practices often dictate that D&O limits of liability be preserved from depletion by non-D&O exposures. On the other hand, many smaller and mid-size companies feel that the chances are remote of getting both a significant D&O claim and a significant EPL claim in the same policy period, therefore they prefer to share a single limit between the two coverages in order to economize. This is a decision that must be made in light of the specific considerations applicable to each insured's situation.

Another important consideration is how the EPL coverage interacts with the D&O policy's Insured vs. Insured exclusion. Some policy forms grant coverage for an EPL claim by an employee or applicant against any insured, while others have specific exceptions, such as excluding EPL claims against directors. It's important to understand the specific EPL coverage granted in a D&O policy, especially if it's going to be an insured's only form of EPL coverage. If an insured entity buys a stand-alone EPL policy, it's also possible, and often prudent, to make the EPL coverage granted by the D&O policy specifically excess of the stand-alone EPL policy's limit of liability. This can be accomplished through the use of an endorsement.

Underwriting EPL can be a tricky task. The standard process involves reviewing the application and employee handbook of the applicant and assessing factors such as the number of employees, average salaries, past claims history, the company's geographic location(s), industry niche and related information. However, there's nothing quite as valuable as a site visit. With a visit one can gauge, at least somewhat, the general morale of the workforce and other important factors such as the diversification of the workforce by age, sex and race. As mentioned previously, employees in the Midwest (this generally doesn't apply on the East Coast or West Coast for some reason, save for Willis) frequently wear company lapel pins when they're happy and proud to be employed with that organization. I have no statistical data to back it, but whenever I saw an office where the majority of the employees were wearing lapel pins and appeared to be happy, I felt it was a good EPL write – assuming the other basic factors all measured up, of course. This is where the "art" of professional lines underwriting comes in; it's something that can't be captured on an underwriting worksheet.

Conversely, one can also pick up negative information during an on-site visit. Once, while being given a tour of a large financial institution's headquarters in the South by its risk manager, my colleague and I noticed a large number of young and physically attractive women in the risk management department. My colleague said something to the effect of "Your office environment is certainly not hard on the eyes."

The risk manager replied, "Yeah, I had to stop hiring so many hot women because guys were coming over to my department from all over the company to get a look. It eventually became too embarrassing."

It probably won't surprise you to learn that we intentionally quoted a very high EPL premium on the next renewal in order to price ourselves out of that risk. I don't know if the company ever had an EPL claim based on the risk manager's hiring practices, but we weren't sticking around to find out.

Insured/Insured Person

Common sense tells us that in a Directors and Officers Liability insurance policy, the Insureds are going to be, at a minimum, the directors and officers of the company buying the policy. The wording typically states that coverage applies to "*the past, present and future duly elected or appointed directors and officers...*" of the company. This can be modified, however, when the applicant business is organized in another form. For example, when dealing with limited liability companies, you'd want members of the board of managers covered, and when dealing with business trusts, you'd want the individual trustees covered. And many insurance carriers will include within the definition of Insureds people holding a position equivalent to a director or officer in any foreign (i.e. non-U.S.) jurisdiction. The basic idea is always to cover the people who are managing the company.

Some carriers try to curry favor with risk managers and general counsels by also specifically naming those positions as insureds. My theory is that this is done because the risk manager and general counsel of a company frequently decide, or have significant input into the decision of, which carrier is chosen to write the D&O policy. Seeing their job specifically described as an insured position may give these individuals a greater feeling of protection. Carriers are not above this seemingly transparent ploy, in my opinion, if it translates into additional business.

The company itself is usually an insured in two respects. First, it receives coverage under Insuring Agreement

B when it advances covered costs to an insured individual for reimbursable claims. After the insured company pays these costs, the insurance carrier reimburses the company for all portions thereof that are covered.

Second, the corporate entity receives coverage under Insuring Agreement C, Securities Claim Entity Coverage, when it's named as a defendant in a suit alleging wrongdoing with respect to the company's securities (assuming, of course, that such an insuring agreement is present in the policy). Many carriers expand the definition of Insured under Insuring Agreement C to include employees below the officer and director level when they're named as a co-defendant in a securities lawsuit, although this is somewhat of an illusory enhancement, for the most part, since very rarely are lower-level employees named as defendants in securities claims. Still, it's an enhancement worth having since it's normally free.

A danger inherent in expanding the definition of Insured too far, which many people overlook, is that this term also comes into play with respect to the policy's Insured vs. Insured exclusion. Every additional person who is defined as an Insured is another person who could, theoretically, bring a claim that would be excluded as being a case of one Insured suing another. Thus, insureds should carefully consider what additional parties they'd like to classify as "Insureds" under their D&O policy before making such requests.

Interrelated Wrongful Acts

Not all carriers include this exact term in the Definitions section of their D&O policy, but the majority of carriers seek to accomplish, in some way, the same objectives as those who use the specific words "Interrelated Wrongful Acts." Some carriers, for example, prefer to use the defined term "Related Claims." The intent is the same, although those carriers get to the result in a different way.

The term Interrelated Wrongful Acts is usually assigned a meaning such as "*two or more Wrongful Acts arising out of the same, related or similar facts, events, circumstances, situations, transactions or occurrences*." The language differs from policy to policy, but the idea is the same: To tie together claims that arise from related wrongful acts so that they may be classified as a single claim. Three main implications arise from this grouping together of related wrongful acts and related claims.

First, many D&O policies have a Prior Acts Exclusion (which gives rise to a Continuity Date, but we'll get into that later). This serves to exclude from coverage any claims arising from wrongful acts that occurred prior to a specified date. By introducing the concept of Interrelated Wrongful Acts, carriers tie actions back to the date of the first occurrence of such Interrelated Wrongful Acts, which sometimes allows them to deny a claim that might otherwise have been covered.

By way of example, let's assume that ABC Corporation's D&O policy has a prior acts date of January 1, 2000. On July 1, 2000 shareholders file a securities class action against the company for alleged misrepresentations contained in a news release dated March 1, 2000. However, those same alleged misrepresentations were also contained in an annual report filed by ABC Corporation on December 1, 1999. The D&O insurer would most likely say that because the alleged misrepresentations were first made in December of 1999, the subsequent misrepresentations in March of 2000 would relate back (because they constitute Interrelated Wrongful Acts) and, thus, the claim would be excluded from coverage by the combination of the Prior Acts Exclusion and the definition of Interrelated Wrongful Acts. Absent a definition of Interrelated Wrongful Acts, the insured could simply take the position that the claim arose from a news release distributed on March 1, 2000 – after the Prior Acts Exclusion date – and, thus, it should be eligible for coverage. The carrier's perspective on this, many times, is that it can't possibly underwrite coverage for every act that a company has taken since its inception (assuming it has been around for a while), thus it must set a reasonable time limitation on covering claims arising from acts occurring before a certain date. Of course, statutes of limitations may also come into play to bar claims brought long after the underlying acts occurred.

The second implication involves actual claims, not merely interrelated wrongful acts. In some situations, insurers only exclude from coverage new claims that are related to prior claims (i.e. Related Claims), which is a higher standard (and better for the insured) than just tying the exclusion back to prior Interrelated Wrongful Acts. If the prior Interrelated

Wrongful Acts didn't give rise to an actual claim before the starting date for covered acts, then the new claim would be eligible for coverage.

The third impact of Interrelated Wrongful Acts has to do with the D&O policy's self-insured retention. If all claims arising out of the same Interrelated Wrongful Acts are considered one claim, first made on the date of the filing of the earliest of such claims, then it's only fair that a single retention be applied to all related claims, as opposed to applying a separate retention for each. This, obviously, works in the insured's favor. But, on the flip side of that, where Interrelated Wrongful Acts give rise to claims in separate policy periods, only one limit of liability will apply to all such claims. So the benefit of only having to satisfy one retention comes with the downside of only having one limit of liability available to respond to the claim.

Loss

Ah, the definition of Loss, one of the all-time favorites among carriers. As any seasoned D&O professional knows, the definition of Loss is largely another exclusion section, albeit not labeled as such. In other words, carriers define Loss more by telling you what it *isn't* rather than by telling you what it *is*.

Most D&O policies are in agreement that Loss shall include "*settlements, damages, judgments (including pre- and post-judgment interest on covered verdict amounts), defense costs and any attorneys' fees of the claimant's that may be awarded in connection with a covered claim.*" After that, we get into the meat of the definition. Below are some elements of loss (the lowercase "l" being intentional) that many D&O policies will exclude from the definition of Loss, followed by suggestions as to how a savvy insured (and her broker) may negotiate a "softening" or liberalization of these provisions to provide greater coverage:

- *Taxes, fines and penalties* - Some carriers will provide coverage for certain fines and penalties that are assessed directly against individuals and that are not reimbursable by the company – provided it's allowed by law;

- *Amounts for which the insureds are not legally liable -* Since the D&O form is a liability policy, there shouldn't be coverage when there is no liability, thus, generally, this provision doesn't need amending;

- *The multiplied portion of multiplied damages* - Some carriers will agree to cover one or two times the amount of the judgment as a multiplied damage penalty, but three times is much rarer;

- *Matters which may be deemed uninsurable pursuant to the law under which the policy is construed* - Most carriers will offer a "most favorable jurisdiction" enhancement, either in their standard policy form or by endorsement. This provision agrees to construe the governing law of payment of the claim to be the most favorable to the insured as long as it has some reasonable connection to the claim, e.g. the jurisdiction in which the claim arose or in which the insured company is headquartered. Sometimes this clause is silent as to how the most favorable venue is determined so from an insured's perspective it's always best to include specific language that grants the insured the right to choose such venue;

- *Clean-up costs related to pollution and hazardous materials* - Some carriers will agree to provide this coverage under the D&O policy's A-Side if an individual insured is personally liable for clean-up costs and such costs cannot be reimbursed by the insured company;

- *Employment-related benefits (e.g. salaries, bonuses, retirement benefits, etc.)* - Carriers will usually not agree to pay these obligations; they're viewed as a cost of doing business for the insured company. Also, many carriers don't consider them to be a true element of Loss since the insured company received the benefit of the employee's services;

- *So-called "bump up" costs* (usually defined as the amount by which a company must increase the price it paid for the shares of a company it acquired. So, for example, if Insured Company A bought Company B for $10 per share and Company B shareholders obtained a judgment declaring that Company B's shares were really worth $12 per share at the time, then the extra $2 per share that Company A would be forced to pay would constitute a bump-up cost) - Carriers will generally not agree to pay the additional amount under the theory that there was no Loss because the shares were received by the insured company and now they're just squaring up by paying the true value, but many carriers will provide defense-cost coverage for these allegations;

- *Costs incurred to comply with injunctive or non-monetary relief* - You might be able to negotiate a sub-limit for this; it's worth a try;

- *Amounts spent in investigating and/or defending a matter which does not constitute a Claim at the time that such costs were incurred (regardless of whether that matter subsequently evolves into a Claim or if those costs also benefit the defense of a covered Claim)* - Many carriers offer coverage, usually subject to a sub-limit, for costs incurred in investigating a matter before it becomes a Claim, including regulatory investigations, "informal investigations" and, especially, the investigation of matters pertaining to a shareholder derivative demand; and

- *Any amounts allocated to non-covered Loss in a situation where a Claim involves both covered and non-covered costs* - Coverage for this is generally not obtainable.

Depending on the particular policy, the definition of Loss may exclude other things as well, but these are most of the major exclusions you'll find in the definition. The key point, however, is to always read the definition of Loss closely because it is a critical component of the policy's overall coverage.

Organization

This term generally refers to the insured entity, although other terms sometimes used for this purpose include Company (which is also the term used to designate the insurer in some policies) Corporation, Named Corporation, Insured Entity and, simply, Insured. This definition, among other things, often sets forth the terms of coverage for subsidiaries, usually by incorporating by reference the term "Subsidiary" as it's defined elsewhere in the policy. Carriers today generally provide automatic coverage for newly created or acquired companies (and their directors and officers) for the remainder of the policy period as long as their assets don't exceed a specified percentage (usually ranging between 10 percent and 25 percent) of the total consolidated assets of the insured Organization on the date of such creation or acquisition. This number, like virtually every provision discussed in this book, can be altered by an endorsement to the policy depending upon the circumstances involved.

Usually, carriers will not grant any coverage for claims arising from acts relating to a new subsidiary that occurred prior to the creation or acquisition of such new subsidiaries. If the new company exceeds the asset threshold set forth in the policy, the carrier will normally grant automatic coverage for only a short period of time (typically 60 or 90 days) while a full underwriting of the new entity occurs and the carrier decides if it wants to offer ongoing coverage and, if so, at what terms, conditions and possible additional premium. It's critical for insureds to notify their D&O carrier(s) of any new subsidiaries in a timely manner because a failure to do so may result in a lapse of coverage for the new entity and its directors and officers after the specified automatic period, especially if the pre-set asset limit is exceeded.

Securities Claim

The definition of a Securities Claim is important because it establishes the D&O policy's coverage under the Entity Securities Coverage Insuring Agreement (colloquially known as "Coverage C") when the insured company finds itself on the receiving end of a Claim involving its securities. Exact definitions vary throughout the industry, but, generally, a Securities Claim is defined as a Claim:

- *Brought against any Insured by a security holder of the Company in his or her capacity as such with respect to their interests in securities of the Company, including derivative actions brought to enforce the rights of the Company; or*

- *Based upon, arising out of attributable to the actual or alleged violation of any federal, state, local or foreign regulation, rule or statute governing securities (including the purchase or sale or offer to purchase or sell such securities) when made in connection with the securities of the Company (including actions brought by the U.S. Securities and Exchange Commission or any other claimant).*

Almost all carriers will exclude from coverage, either directly in the definition of a Securities Claim or in the Exclusions section of the policy, disputes between the Company and any past, present or future employees over the insured Company's offer, grant or issuance of stock options, stock warrants and any other securities. Basically, carriers want to avoid picking up employee compensation claims under a D&O policy. In the early days of corporate Securities Claim coverage, this issue was not contemplated, and carriers found themselves getting dragged into stock-option battles that they had no intent of covering when they drafted their policies. Thus, the explicit compensation Claim exclusion was born. However, coverage is generally available, to some degree, for these types of Claims under an Employment Practices Liability (EPL) policy.

Wrongful Act

The definition of this term is critical in any D&O Insurance policy. When you boil it down, a D&O Insurance purchaser is simply buying coverage for Claims arising from Wrongful Acts. It's not exactly that simple, but close.

Although wordings vary, and some carriers include language dealing with things like Employment Practices Wrongful Acts and Outside Entity Wrongful Acts, just about every D&O policy intends for a Wrongful Act to encompass *"any actual or alleged breach of duty, neglect, error, misstatement, misleading statement, omission or act by any Insured Person in his respective capacity as such..."* Most policies will then go on to include within this definition "*any other matter claimed against an Insured Person solely by reason of his or her status as such.*"

Wrongful Act will also be defined, with respect to the Insured Entity under Coverage C, as including a Wrongful Act arising from a securities violation.

Typically, there's not much tweaking that occurs with this definition. Occasionally, insureds may request inclusion of language that specifies that a Wrongful Act will include "deliberate" acts, although many carriers will push back and say that the concept is already understood to be in the definition.

***

It can't be stressed enough that the Definitions section is a critical component of any D&O Insurance policy; it must be reviewed carefully to fully understand the policy's overall scope of coverage. In addition to the terms reviewed above, there are a number of other defined words and phrases that appear in D&O Insurance policies on the market today, such as "Extradition Costs," "Financial Impairment," "Liberty Protection Costs," "Outside Entity Insured Person," and a host of others. The important thing is to know exactly what the carrier intends to cover and how that fits into the insured's needs. Sometimes you'll have to tailor (or "manuscript" as we say in the industry) a definition so that it meets the insured's specific needs. Not every "off the shelf" solution is perfect for every risk.

3. The Exclusions

The Exclusions section of a typical D&O policy can be quite lengthy. This is due, in large part, to the fact that the policy generally covers thc management functions of an insured entity. There are a lot of potential liabilities attaching to the management of a company, especially a large publicly traded company, and, thus, D&O carriers must restrict their coverage grants to just the discrete universe of what they consider to be acceptable – and insurable – risks.

Carriers try to avoid having to resort to double-lettering their exclusions once they pass "Z," the 26th exclusion, by inserting exclusions into other parts of the policy, such as the Definitions section (as mentioned above). Most carriers seem to believe that it doesn't look insured-friendly for a policy to have Exclusions designated as AA, BB, CC, etc.

In this section we'll review (in alphabetical order) some of the major exclusions found in D&O policies and explain their significance. We'll also examine how some can be reasonably altered to provide a measure of additional coverage for the insured without totally compromising the carrier's underwriting integrity.

Bodily Injury and Property Damage

A standard exclusion in virtually every D&O Insurance policy, this provision excludes from coverage losses that would more traditionally be covered by a Comprehensive General Liability (CGL) policy or another insurance policy. Sometimes, exceptions ("carve-backs") are provided to cover bodily injury damages allegedly suffered as a consequence of a covered wrongful act, such as an employment practices violation or a securities claim wrongful act. The bodily injury claim carve-back usually results in coverage for ancillary harm, such as anxiety or insomnia caused by an otherwise covered act. For example, a claimant may allege in a securities claim that because he lost his life savings when the insured's stock price dropped, he now suffers from insomnia, migraine headaches and other physical maladies.

Employee Compensation and Labor Law Liability

This exclusion addresses employee compensation issues. It clarifies that the D&O policy is not a backstop to cover the insured company's liability for things such as back wages, overtime and other employee compensation and benefits. Usually, the exclusion will state that the policy doesn't apply to actual or alleged violations of a variety of specific employment laws, such as the Fair Labor Standards Act, the Consolidated Omnibus Budget Reconciliation Act (COBRA), the Worker Adjustment and Retraining Notification (WARN) Act and the Occupational Health and Safety Act (OSHA), as well as any similar local, state, federal or foreign laws. A carve-back is usually provided for allegations that would otherwise be covered under the D&O policy's grant of employment practices coverage.

So-called "wage and hour" claims have increased in frequency in recent years. These generally allege that an employer unfairly withheld compensation from its employees by doing such things as not paying overtime that was due or by forcing employees to work "off the clock." Carriers have been seeking ways to address this growing issue and some now provide defense cost coverage for these claims, often with a sub-limit of liability well below the policy's overall limit. Stay tuned as other creative solutions evolve to address wage and hour losses.

ERISA

The ERISA exclusion in a D&O policy is intended to avoid coverage for any claims arising from the Employee Retirement Income Security Act of 1974 and any amendments thereto. Most D&O carriers, if not all, sell separate Fiduciary Liability Insurance policies that cover the trustees of ERISA plans and, thus, the insurers don't want to pick up any liabilities associated with ERISA violations under their D&O policies. Basically, what carriers are saying here is: "Buy our ERISA policy and leave this one alone."

Errors and Omissions (E&O)

Insurers don't want to provide coverage under a D&O policy for claims arising from errors and omissions committed by insureds in the course of their dealings with their customers or clients. Carriers generally take the position that the purpose of a D&O policy is to protect insureds against claims arising from their management of the insured entity. These are typically brought by shareholders (or other investors), employees, regulators and others with an interest in how the insured entity is managed. E&O claims, on the other hand, emanate from third-party customers or clients whose main interest is in the quality of goods or services provided by the insured. And, coincidentally, most D&O carriers also sell separate E&O policies (requiring, of course, the payment of separate premiums) that more adequately address E&O issues.

There are some exceptions to this general rule of excluding E&O claims under a D&O policy.

One is known as the "failure to supervise" carve-back with respect to securities claims. This extends coverage under the D&O policy when management's failure to properly supervise the insured company's provision of professional services to customers or clients causes such significant losses that the company's stock price drops and results in a securities class action. An example of this would be where a bank repeatedly commits negligence in the mortgage-lending process and is forced to pay a gigantic settlement to customers that results in a severe drop in the bank's stock price. One could argue that the resulting securities claim originated from an E&O claim, but with the securities claim carve-back this would not be an issue since coverage would be granted.

Another exception is usually granted for E&O claims that implicate the D&O policy under the employment practices extension. For example, many employment practices coverage grants in D&O policies include coverage for, among other things, discrimination claims. If a customer of a bank were to allege that he was charged a higher interest rate than other bank customers because he was a minority, this claim could be covered under the employment practices extension even though it originated with a professional service to a customer of the bank.

A number of carriers, seeking to limit the number of exclusions appearing in their basic D&O policy form, do not have an E&O exclusion in their standard D&O policy but rather attach it by endorsement when insuring a company that provides professional services.

Fraud/Criminal Acts

The exclusion pertaining to fraudulent activities falls within the ambit of what's known as "the conduct exclusions." These are exclusions that apply to claims arising out of the conduct of individual insureds.

A typical Fraud exclusion will state that it applies to any claim "...alleging, based upon, arising out of or attributable to any deliberately fraudulent or criminal act, error or omission by the insured." Most Fraud exclusions on today's market are conditioned upon a <u>final adjudication</u> of said fraud. That is, a mere allegation of fraud won't be sufficient to trigger the exclusion, it actually has to be proved by a "final adjudication." Many Fraud exclusions will also provide that if any insured is found liable of fraud, then any defense costs that have been advanced by the insurer to that insured must be repaid to the carrier.

There are a few points to be aware of here. First, in earlier days the word "deliberate" did not always appear in this exclusion. Fraud is a deliberate act – the person committing the fraud must intend to defraud someone else, it doesn't happen by accident – and, thus, the word "deliberate" is unnecessary. But, nonetheless, adding "deliberate" gives some insureds an added measure of comfort with the belief that it somehow narrows the exclusion.

Second, "final adjudication" language is preferable, from an insured's perspective, to "in fact" wording that has also been widely used. Some insureds fear that a sworn statement offered during a deposition or at trial alleging that fraud has been committed could be construed as establishing an "in fact" instance of fraud. Most carriers probably would not take that position, but in order to assuage insureds, many D&O policies now use "final adjudication" wording. Of course, for the sake of precision one must know what exactly constitutes a "final adjudication." Can it only be established by a court of competent jurisdiction, or can binding arbitration also count? Some policies also state that if an insured issues a sworn statement confessing that he committed fraud, that's also sufficient to trigger the fraud exclusion.

Third, there's the issue of paying back advanced defense costs in the event of a finding of fraud. Usually defendants found guilty of fraud have lost (or are about to lose) substantially all of their assets. In my 20-plus years in the insurance industry, I don't recall ever seeing a carrier successfully recover previously advanced defense costs, but I guess it can happen. However, if I were an insured, I would try to get this clause negotiated out of the policy.

When I was at D'Amato & Lynch in the late 1980s, I was assigned to handle a coverage matter involving allegations of fraud for one of our carrier clients. The insured was an oil and gas limited partnership in Oklahoma. "This should be fairly easy," I thought to myself upon first looking at the underlying complaint. "The fraud exclusion should take care of this. We'll just issue a declination."

Back in those days, the fraud exclusion was considerably broader than today; it applied in most instances to mere allegations of fraud. However, I received a rude awakening when I reviewed the policy and learned that the underwriter had agreed to remove the fraud exclusion in exchange for a fairly nominal additional premium. Our client eventually paid a loss of nearly a million dollars.

Lesson: When an insured requests removal of the fraud exclusion, it should be a major red flag. Insureds generally know their exposures better than anyone. If they think fraud is a real concern, they're probably right.

Illegal Personal Profit or Advantage

Insurance carriers don't want to indemnify insureds who obtain some type of personal profit or advantage (including insider trading profits) to which they were not legally entitled. In many jurisdictions, this would be against public policy anyway, and where it isn't, reimbursing such losses would seem to encourage – or at least support – illegal activity. Besides not wanting to lose claims dollars, insurance carriers use this exclusion because they don't want the publicity of being known as the company that provided restitution to a bad actor who gained an illegal profit and was forced to disgorge it by a court.

Many carriers today provide a carve-back that only triggers this exclusion when a final adjudication (sometimes specified to be non-appealable) establishes the existence of the illegal personal profit or gain. Some carriers (but not many in today's market) take a broader approach by making their exclusion apply to any claim "based upon, alleging, arising out of or in any way related to" an illegal personal profit or gain without any further qualification.

Carriers have also applied the illegal personal profit or advantage exclusion when the existence of such illegal profit or advantage has merely been proven "in fact." This is considered a lower standard of proof than a "final adjudication." For example, an insured could confess under oath to receiving an illegal profit. This would not legally constitute a "final adjudication" by itself, but a carrier might say that a sworn statement by the insured constitutes a "fact." Because of the uncertainty that this can create, the majority of carriers have moved away from the "in fact" standard; however, at least one carrier specifically identifies a sworn confession as being sufficient to trigger the illegal profit or gain exclusion.

A few years ago, controversy ignited in the D&O world when some carriers started applying the illegal personal profit or gain exclusion to the proceeds of public securities offerings if a court later ruled that such proceeds were illegally received under the Securities Act of 1933. Arguments ran both ways as to whether this was a proper application of the exclusion and some people said that if it was, a substantial portion of the value of a D&O policy would be negated. Today, some carriers provide an explicit carve-back to this exclusion to confirm that it doesn't apply to actual or alleged violations of Sections 11, 12 and 15 (or some combination thereof) of the Securities Act of 1933.

Inadequate or Excessive Consideration

This is also known informally as the "Bump Up Exclusion." It's intended to prevent the carrier from having to pay off shareholders in a mergers and acquisitions situation, whether because the insured is accused of paying too little or too much for the acquired company. (Frequently, an insured faces both accusations, albeit contradictory, after an acquisition.) We've covered this already, but it's worth reviewing again. An example of the typical scenario would be where the insured buys Company A for $10 a share. The shareholders of Company A, feeling cheated, file a suit alleging that Company A was really worth $15 per share. If a court agrees with the shareholders, it can force the insured to pay an additional $5 per share for Company A.

The purpose of the Inadequate or Excessive Consideration exclusion is to ensure that the carrier doesn't have to pay this extra $5 per share to "bump up" the sale price on behalf of its insured under the D&O policy. Similarly, if shareholders of the insured believe that Company A was only worth $5 per share and that the insured overpaid and wasted shareholder assets, the shareholders may sue the directors and officers of the insured to recover the alleged $5 per share overpayment. This exclusion applies to either scenario; whether an underpayment or overpayment is alleged, the carrier does not want to be liable for correcting the situation. However, many carriers will provide defense costs when such allegations are made. In addition, some carriers have crafted carve-backs to this exclusion to provide coverage when a reputable investment bank has reviewed the proposed transaction and has issued a written opinion that the price paid for the target company was fair and adequate. As the market firms up, concessions like this tend to go away.

Insured vs. Insured (also known as "One v. One")

This exclusion came about, according to D&O Insurance lore (which, in this case, I believe is fairly reliable), after Bank of America ("BofA") purchased Seattle's Seafirst Bank in 1983. Sometime after the purchase was consummated, BofA discovered what it believed to be negligence on the part of some Seafirst Bank managers. BofA sued the former Seafirst Bank managers, who were now employees of BofA. The defendants sought coverage under BofA's D&O policy. Until that point, it seems, no insurer had expected that an insured company would sue its own managers and, thus, no Insured vs. Insured exclusion was contained in any D&O policies at the time. It's my belief that this case was the catalyst for the creation of the Insured vs. Insured exclusion.

The main purpose of the Insured vs. Insured Exclusion is to prevent collusive suits between company insiders, although that's not its only purpose. Some carriers use the Insured vs. Insured Exclusion to withhold coverage from claims brought by deep-pocketed plaintiffs (such as regulators) in a situation where such plaintiffs attempt to step into the shoes of an insured to bring a claim that might otherwise never have come to fruition. These carriers might say, for example, that actuarially they didn't price the policy to cover these types of claims. And, of course, as with just about everything else in this book, specific policy wording and underlying facts govern any actual claim situation so don't hold me to the above!

It's not hard to imagine, with respect to collusive claims, a situation where two directors of a failing company get together and say "Look, we have $50 million in D&O Insurance coverage. You sue me for making the bad business decisions that led to this mess and after I admit wrongdoing, we'll get a big check from the insurance company which we'll use to get the company back on its feet."

Despite insurers' concerns of collusive lawsuits among insureds, today's D&O policies nonetheless contain a number of carve-backs to the Insured vs. Insured exclusion which expand coverage and limit the application of the exclusion. Some of these include exceptions for derivative claims, claims brought in the name of the insured company by bankruptcy trustees, regulators or liquidators, claims brought by a former director who hasn't served on the insured company's board for a specified minimum number of years (usually three or four), and claims brought by insureds in the form of a cross-claim, counter-claim or third-party claim – as long as the underlying claim is otherwise covered.

The Insured vs. Insured exclusion is one that carriers generally don't like to alter in any material way (besides those noted above) because it always raises a red flag, causing carriers to ask, "What does this insured know about potential claims by insureds against other insureds?" And insurers will sometimes ask policyholders "Why would you want your policy depleted by infighting? Its limits of liability are meant to protect you against outside threats."

Non-Monetary and/or Injunctive Relief

This exclusion used to be standard in D&O policies, but that has changed in recent years. While some carriers still use an explicit exclusion for non-monetary and/or injunctive relief in their D&O policies, others bury the exclusion in the definition of "Loss." Still others, interestingly (interesting to me anyway, and probably you too since you're reading this book!), make no clear effort to exclude this type of loss.

One rationale that carriers use for not providing coverage for non-monetary loss is that it is difficult to quantify such damages and, thus, there's a greater potential for a coverage dispute between the insurer and insured. For example, let's say a company's board of directors was ordered to provide handicap ramps at all company locations. One could easily see how a dispute would arise over which contractor(s) to use, what quality of materials to use, how many ramps to install, etc.

The two areas where carriers are most concerned about paying for loss in the form of non-monetary relief seem to be: 1) Compliance with Americans with Disabilities Act (ADA) mandates (as in the handicapped ramp example above); and 2) The cleanup of pollution. Both of these activities have the potential to be quite costly and, carriers will say, are not within the contemplation of the coverage of a traditional D&O policy. However, many carriers will make an exception to the pollution exclusion by granting an A-Side carve-back to provide coverage for pollution remediation costs when the insured entity can't reimburse individual insureds and these individuals have personal liability for the cleanup.

Outside Directorship Liability (ODL)

Companies sometimes ask their directors and/or officers to serve as a director of an outside entity. For example, assume that DogFoodCo, a dog-food manufacturer, asks one if its directors, Mr. Smith, to serve on the board of the ASPCA because it's good for community relations. Mr. Smith gets sued for something that he does in connection with the ASPCA, but the plaintiff also names DogFoodCo as a defendant since it asked Mr. Smith to serve on the board. (Also, the plaintiff is motivated to sue DogFoodCo because he probably believes that DogFoodCo has deeper pockets than the ASPCA.) An insurer would use the ODL exclusion to prevent its policy from responding to the lawsuit against Mr. Smith and the ASPCA in this example. One could argue that Mr. Smith's service on the ASPCA board was part of his duties as a director of DogFoodCo since it was in DogFoodCo's interests for him to serve on the ASPCA's board and DogFoodCo requested that he do so, thus he should be covered under DogFoodCo's D&O policy. However, the carrier would say that it uses a blanket exclusion for all ODL situations because otherwise it would have to review and underwrite the corporate governance procedures, financial status and other key factors for all outside organizations on which its insured's directors and officers might serve.

Like many things in the insurance world, there are exceptions to the ODL exclusion.

Many carriers will provide blanket ODL coverage to individual insureds when they are serving on the board of a not-for-profit 501(c)(3) organization, as defined by the U.S. Internal Revenue Code, as well as certain other types of non-for-profit organizations (again, you'd need to check the specific policy to see what it covers). By "blanket" coverage, we mean that it's automatically granted and doesn't need to be individually underwritten because the coverage is built-in to the D&O policy.

Carriers may also provide an ODL extension of coverage to individual insureds serving on the boards of non-501(c)(3) organizations after underwriting the exposure on an individual basis. The insurer may ask for things such as the outside entity's financials, a copy of its bylaws, copies of its

D&O Insurance policy(ies) and other pertinent information. If an insurer decides to grant the non-501(c)(3) ODL coverage, whether for a for-profit entity or another type of non-profit, under its D&O policy, it is likely to do so in one of two ways. This is one of the most frequently confused concepts in D&O Insurance, so take a swig of your energy drink and pay close attention here!

The first coverage grant option is called "Double Excess ODL." Sticking with our example above, this would mean that the ODL coverage under DogFoodCo's D&O policy would only be triggered for a claim arising from Mr. Smith's service on the ASPCA's board after: 1) The ASPCA's D&O coverage responds to the claim and the limit of liability is exhausted by payment of covered loss; _and_ 2) The ASPCA either becomes insolvent and can't reimburse Mr. Smith or it's prevented from legally doing so.

"Triple Excess ODL" coverage would respond in this situation after the same two factors as above, but then a third requirement would have to be met: DogFoodCo would need to reimburse Mr. Smith directly out of its own coffers – unless it becomes insolvent or is prevented by law from doing so. Once all three of those conditions are met, then Triple Excess ODL coverage would respond under DogFoodCo's D&O policy.

Many people feel that Triple Excess ODL is worth very little since three substantial triggers must be satisfied in order to activate the coverage but, nonetheless, many insureds are happy to have it, especially since there is usually no charge or only a small charge associated with this enhancement (if it's not already built-in to the policy).

It's important that brokers and insureds be aware that the main insured's D&O policy (DogFoodCo in our example above) most likely won't follow form of the outside entity's D&O policy. Thus, a claim that's covered under the outside entity's D&O policy may run up against an exclusion in the main company's D&O form. Prudent insureds and their brokers will compare the two policies side-by-side to determine if there are any significant gaps in coverage that need to be addressed, such as by possibly getting the D&O insurer of the main company to agree to be completely follow-form of the outside entity's D&O policy.

Pending or Prior Proceeding

An old saw in the insurance industry is that carriers won't write a policy on a burning house. Or, as some people say, *"You can't buy a homeowner's policy when you smell smoke."* The point being, of course, that insurance is meant to cover fortuitous events, those happening by accident or chance, not those that are a certainty.

The pending or prior proceeding exclusion imports that concept from the realm of property insurance to professional lines. Because D&O Insurance protects insureds against liability, if a potentially covered liability matter had already been pending at some point before the insured first bought coverage from the current carrier, that carrier will not want to pick up claims that may arise from the prior "burning house."

From the insurer's perspective, this removes the fortuity requirement of insurance.

The exact wording for this exclusion varies from policy to policy – as with most every other provision in the D&O world – but, generally, it will negate coverage for "any Claim alleging, arising out of, related to or based upon any pending or prior written demand, lawsuit or other proceeding pending on or before the date set forth in Item _____ of the Declarations or the same or substantially similar facts, situations or circumstances underlying or alleged in such demand, lawsuit or proceeding." Some pending or prior proceeding exclusions will also knock out coverage for Claims arising from any order, judgment or decree relating to such pending or prior matters.

Generally speaking, this is, in my opinion, a fair exclusion for a D&O policy to contain. Carriers shouldn't be expected to provide coverage for previously known problems. The key here is to have a reasonable interpretation of what is "based upon, alleging or related to" the prior matters. Obviously, insureds want to narrow this exclusion as much as possible, while carriers want to broaden it to the greatest extent.

Carriers will generally provide the "continuity" (i.e. unbroken period of continuous coverage) for pending and prior matters starting after the date they first wrote D&O coverage for a particular insured. For example, assume a covered claim arose two years ago when the carrier was writing D&O for this insured, but it was eventually dismissed. If is the same claim was subsequently resurrected during the current policy period, that same carrier would normally agree to cover the claim and the Pending or Prior Proceeding exclusion would not apply. However, most likely such a resurrected claim would be classified under the previous policy in force when the claim based on the same facts was originally made, either because it would qualify as an "interrelated claim" and/or the original notice would still stand as notice of a potential claim which reverts back to the original policy. As always, specific policy language would govern.

The existence of a Pending and Prior Proceeding exclusion underscores the importance of providing a thorough "laundry list" of potential claims to a carrier when an insured is moving coverage to another insurer. Usually, any matter that's identified with requisite specificity on the laundry list that later evolves into a claim will be said to relate back to the expired policy, thus the Pending and Prior Proceedings exclusion will not be an obstacle to coverage.

Pollution

Insurance carriers are very wary of allowing their D&O policies to serve as "wrap" policies (or as a "backstop") to address liabilities that the D&O policy is not intended to cover. One of these perils is pollution and the often-significant costs associated with clean-ups or remediation. Most D&O policies exclude coverage for any claim alleging, based upon, arising out of or attributable to any actual or alleged pollution problem, including costs associated with testing for, monitoring, cleaning up, containing or neutralizing/detoxifying any pollutants. "Pollution" is almost universally defined in D&O policies to include just about anything even remotely related to the traditional dictionary definition of pollution. Remediation of environmental problems can be exceedingly costly, and carriers generally do not want any involvement with those issues under a D&O policy.

However, as with many rules, there's an exception to this one. Most D&O insurers will provide a carve-back to grant A-Side coverage when a pollution claim is brought directly against a director or officer and no indemnification from the corporate entity is available. This has very rarely happened in practice, but, still, most directors and officers take comfort that this enhancement exists given the potentially astronomical costs involved in pollution situations. Some carriers, however, restrict this A-Side enhancement to only grant coverage for *securities claims* arising from a pollution situation, while others do not impose such a restriction. Additionally, some carriers provide a carve-back to cover whistle-blower claims arising from a pollution problem.

4. Miscellaneous Sections

The average D&O policy has a number of additional sections that form an important part of the policy and shouldn't be overlooked. Let's take a look at some of the more important of these miscellaneous sections.

Action Against The Insurer

This is a part of the D&O policy that carriers hope never comes into play. It addresses coverage disputes between the insured and insurer. These clauses do not always hold up in court.

Many policies keep this section relatively short, setting forth two main points.

First, they state that no action can be taken against the carrier unless the insureds have fully complied with all terms of the policy. There are many provisions of the typical D&O Insurance policy that require compliance by the insureds (e.g. they must submit complete and 100 percent accurate information with their application, provide full cooperation and assistance in the event of a claim, etc.), thus, it's usually not too hard for a carrier – if they desire – to find one or two issues on which there has been less than full compliance by insureds. But if those issues are not relevant or significant enough, chances are a court would ignore them when interpreting this provision.

The second point states that no third party has the right to join the carrier as a party in an action against an insured to determine the insured's liability. This provision also usually says that insureds themselves are also not allowed to drag the carrier directly into a case (known as "impleading") against an insured. But whether such a provision is enforceable against a third-party plaintiff who was never a party to the D&O policy is another issue, usually one determined by applicable law, not simply what the policy says.

Some carriers try to restrict insureds' options for resolving coverage disputes against the carrier to some form of alternative dispute resolution (ADR) process, such as mediation or arbitration. There are two main reasons for this. First, ADR is usually a much less expensive way to resolve disputes than full-blown litigation, which can involve things such as multiple lawyers conducting protracted discovery and filing numerous briefs and motions – all of which cost a lot of money. Second, and this may be the main motivator for many carriers, ADR proceedings generally do not allow for an award of punitive damages. Paying the policy limit in a disputed matter is bad enough from a carrier's perspective, but the prospect of paying a large punitive damages award – one with no pre-set ceiling – is much worse, and every carrier fears it.

Allocation

As you've no doubt discerned by now, no section of a D&O Insurance policy is uniform throughout the industry. Some policies, for example, will subsume the allocation discussion within the Defense and Settlement section (or elsewhere). And just about every other key section of a D&O policy is similarly subject to the industry's mix-and-match approach to drafting. Standardized industry policy forms aren't used in the D&O market and probably never will be.

A D&O policy's Allocation Clause governs the allocation of defense costs and/or loss payments which generally arises in two situations. The first is when insureds incur defense costs and/or other covered loss (such as a settlement payment) jointly with one or more other parties who are not insureds under the applicable D&O policy. The other situation occurs when a claim involves both covered and uncovered allegations against one or more insureds.

The allocation between covered and uncovered loss under a D&O policy is possibly the most negotiated – and sometimes litigated – issue when settling a claim.

Back when I was practicing law in the prehistoric days of D&O Insurance (the late 1980s), we used a rather simple allocation analysis on behalf of our insurance-carrier clients when insureds and non-insureds were being defended in a single claim by the same counsel. It's almost embarrassing to recount the methodology here, but it serves as a valuable illustration of how the industry used to operate and how it has evolved.

Let's assume a lawsuit was filed against two insured and three uninsured individuals. We'd argue that our client, the D&O carrier, was only liable for two-fifths (or 40 percent) of the total defense costs using a pro rata analysis. However, in the same scenario, if three defendants were our client's insureds and two were not, we'd say, "Look, there are two classes of defendants here, the insureds and the uninsureds, so our client will pay 50 percent of the defense costs, it's only fair." Yes, we were playing both sides of the street, or trying to anyway. Usually that would only be an opening gambit and further negotiations would take place before a final allocation was agreed upon.

Today, in such a situation many individual insureds demand their own counsel, separate from the uninsured defendants' counsel. They point to the possibility of a conflict of interest as one of the main justifications for this. Insurers will often agree to such an arrangement either because of specific wording in their policy or just to be user-friendly. And in some instances, insured individuals each want their own law firms defending them even when they have no apparent conflicts with insured co-defendants. Specific policy wordings may govern this issue, but it can also be negotiated at the time that it arises if it hasn't been pre-addressed in the policy.

D&O Insurance has undergone an evolutionary process since the late 1980s with respect to addressing the allocation issue. Some of the developments were dictated by court decisions while others were "solutions" introduced by carriers themselves.

Allocation under D&O policies was frequently a problem in the 1980s and early 1990s when both the corporate entity and individual directors and officers were named as defendants in a securities class action. Without getting into too much legal minutia here, suffice it to say that in 1995 a ruling by the Ninth Circuit of the U.S. Court of Appeals in a case brought by the department store Nordstrom created something called "the larger settlement rule." This ruling essentially required D&O carriers to pay 100 percent of all settlements in most cases (if not all) where both individual insured defendants and the uninsured (for its own corporate liability) corporation were defendants. This decision, although only binding on courts within the Ninth Circuit, nonetheless caused great consternation among insurers who felt that they weren't getting adequate premium payments to cover this increased liability. Thus, a new coverage feature was introduced into the market in 1995 by AIG, although it was quickly mimicked by most other carriers (as all good insurance innovations are!): entity coverage for securities claims.

At first insureds could purchase varying percentages of entity coverage for securities claims, e.g. 50 percent, 75 percent, etc., but eventually the market migrated to virtually all insureds purchasing 100 percent entity coverage. This meant that the entity would receive full coverage for its share of corporate liability in any securities class action. The cost for this enhancement was not very significant – in many instances it was thrown in practically for free – but it did greatly reduce the amount of coverage litigation and other discord between carriers and their insureds.

Today, allocation of loss in a claim that is covered to some degree but not necessarily 100 percent is handled in a variety of ways. Most major D&O carriers use wording that says something to the effect of "the insureds and the insurer agree to use their best efforts to determine a fair and reasonable allocation of Loss as between the insureds and the insurer, taking into account the relative legal and financial exposures of the parties and the relative benefits obtained by each."

Some observers, especially policyholders' coverage counsel, consider the Allocation section of any D&O policy to contain an additional exclusion, and they believe that it should be reviewed closely and negotiated to an acceptable point (and I agree). Carriers adopt different approaches to allocation. Some state that it only applies to settlement/judgment amounts and not to defense costs. Some set forth their formula but then provide for some type of expedited arbitration process to help arrive at a final allocation arrangement if one can't be mutually agreed upon. And there are other variations in this ever-evolving area. The key, as with most other parts of a D&O policy, is to review the language closely and arrive at something that everyone can live with before a claim is made.

Cancellation/Renewal of Coverage

This section, like most provisions in a typical D&O Insurance policy, has evolved over the years (much like your hairstyles since college!) The changes have been generally beneficial to insureds, thanks to longer periods of soft-market conditions that have led to more liberalized coverage terms. Nowadays, many carriers agree that they can only cancel their D&O Insurance policies in the event of the insured's non-payment of the premium. In case of non-payment, carriers usually agree to a 10- or 15-day waiting period after the insured receives written notice of the carrier's intention to cancel before such cancellation becomes effective. This gives the insured a reasonable opportunity to make payment. However, state laws or insurance regulations may override the policy's specific waiting period for cancellation.

Generally, if a state law or regulation is more favorable to the insured than what an insurance policy provides (in any area, not just rules governing cancellation), the state law wins out. Thus, if a carrier offers a 15-day waiting period before cancellation for non-payment of premium but applicable state law requires a 30-day minimum wait, then the policy's provision will be overruled and the insured will have 30 days to pay the premium after it receives notice of the carrier's intention to cancel for non-payment.

The cancellation issue can, at times, be fairly significant in the world of D&O Insurance. This is because some brokerage firms (though certainly not all) earn meaningful revenue from the interest that accumulates in their client escrow accounts. These brokers try to collect premiums from insureds as soon as possible after a policy is bound, but then hold it for as long as possible before paying the carrier. Sometimes these brokers wait a bit too long to remit the premium, thus prompting the insurer to generate a non-payment cancellation notice, which generally is sent directly to both the broker and the insured. If the insured, who assumed that the premium was transmitted to the carrier shortly after the insured paid the broker some time ago, receives a non-payment cancellation notice, it can cause quite a problem for the broker. Thus, it's not uncommon for brokers to call underwriters to plead with them for an extension on the deadline for sending a cancellation notice so the broker has time to remit the premium that's been earning interest in his escrow account. Some jurisdictions have specific laws or regulations governing the treatment of client monies held by insurance brokers. If you're interested in specific laws, please consult an attorney (this book provides NO legal advice!)

Insureds are generally allowed to cancel their policies at any time and for any reason (or no reason at all) under most D&O Insurance policies these days. Some policies state that if either the carrier or the insured cancels the policy, the insured will receive a *pro rata* refund of the unearned portion of the premium based on the days remaining in the original policy period. However, other D&O Insurance policies state that if the insured cancels, it's only entitled to a "short rate" refund, which is calculated differently and provides less of a refund (and more of a penalty) to the insured than a *pro rata* refund. This point is usually negotiable before the policy is bound.

Some carriers that retain the right to cancel a normal one-year D&O policy will nonetheless agree to a non-cancellation clause when binding a three-year D&O policy. Such longer-term policies are usually offered only in soft-market conditions. Carriers offer this non-cancellation feature to incentivize insureds to buy the longer policy in a soft market, thus generating more premium revenue for the carrier. Insureds like this feature on a three-year policy because they want protection against the onset of a sudden hard market that might entice the carrier to cancel the lower-premium policy in order to rewrite it at a higher then-going rate.

Change in Exposure or Control

The old adage "Insurance carriers don't like surprises" comes into play here. When a carrier signs on to write a company's D&O Insurance, it assesses the risks as they exist at the time of the application and crosses its fingers that things won't change much during the course of the policy period. However, when an insured company gets bought or when it purchases or creates a new subsidiary, its D&O Insurance risk profile can change significantly, thus potentially creating an unwanted surprise for the carrier. To guard against this, carriers include specific provisions in their D&O Insurance policies. One such clause usually provides only a limited window of coverage for new subsidiaries, unless their asset size is under a specific threshold, typically a percentage of the insured company's total consolidated assets as of the date of the acquisition/creation. Another provision triggers a total cessation of coverage for claims arising from acts committed after a new owner takes over the company.

The rationale behind this is easy to understand. With respect to subsidiaries, whether newly created by the insured or acquired from another owner, the D&O carrier wants to be sure that it's comfortable with a number of factors, including the type of business conducted by the subsidiary and the competence of its management. For instance, if a tire manufacturer decides to purchase a maker of jet engines, a D&O carrier would probably have serious concerns and would want to underwrite the deal closely before agreeing to add the new subsidiary to the D&O Insurance policy. Among other things, it would want to know why the tire company was getting into the jet-engine business, what long-term plans it had for the new subsidiary and what expertise the current tire-company management might have in overseeing a jet-engine manufacturer. (Note: Just writing about this hypothetical transaction makes the D&O insurer part of my brain nervous!)

The example above is not as far-fetched as you may think. One company insured by an employer of mine started out as a website designer and over time morphed into an aerospace software firm. Drastic changes like this certainly aren't commonplace, but they do occur.

Most D&O Insurance policies today provide an automatic window of coverage for claims arising from acts occurring during some relatively short period of time after an insured company buys or creates a new subsidiary, usually 60 or 90 days. The insured is required to submit relevant underwriting information to the carrier and agree to any additional terms and conditions that the carrier may impose, as well as pay any additional premium that the carrier may require. If the new subsidiary's assets exceed the previously designated threshold, then, theoretically, all bets are off and the carrier can refuse to provide a quote for D&O coverage, although this is rarely done.

Depending upon market conditions, insureds may be successful in getting carriers to increase the asset threshold for subsidiaries to 30 percent or more of the insured parent company's consolidated assets as of the time of the new subsidiary's creation or acquisition. Generally, however, this coverage will only apply to claims arising from acts committed *after* the new entity became a subsidiary, as defined in the policy. This can be an issue for insureds who assume all liabilities of subsidiaries that they purchase from the previous owner. The optimal resolution of this problem is usually the purchase of a separate run-off D&O Insurance policy to cover claims arising from wrongful acts committed before the subsidiary was purchased. One could also build-in this coverage to the ongoing D&O policy for the parent company, but many insureds don't want their D&O Insurance limits of liability eroded by claims arising from acts that took place before they had management control of the new subsidiary.

A change in ownership of an insured parent company presents an even bigger challenge for D&O insurers, and it's one that most don't want to accept, not on a blanket basis anyway. The majority of D&O Insurance policies state that when an insured parent company is acquired, the policy immediately stops covering claims arising from wrongful acts occurring after the date of acquisition. However, many D&O Insurance policies state that they automatically convert to run-off coverage for the remainder of the policy's original term, meaning that they'll provide coverage for claims first made and reported before the policy's original expiration date but only for claims arising from wrongful acts occurring before the acquisition date.

Some carriers, especially in softer market cycles, will also agree in the D&O policy form itself (or, sometimes, via endorsement) to provide automatic run-off quotes of certain lengths with specified caps on the premium. For example, a D&O Insurance policy may state that it can convert to run-off for: 1) one year after the acquisition date for an additional premium of not more than 150 percent of the expiring annual premium; or 2) three years after the acquisition date for an additional premium of not more than 200 percent of the expiring annual premium. Usually these conversion-to-run-off arrangements provide only an extension of the expiring D&O Insurance policy's original limit of liability, not a fresh, unimpaired limit. This may not be a problem when no claims have been reported under the expiring policy, but if there's a chance the expiring limit will be reduced by a previous claim, insureds will most likely want to seek a quote for a fresh limit of liability, usually under an entirely new run-off policy.

It's important to note that I used the phrase "of not more than..." in the sample run-off clause above. This is the preferred language in my opinion (and in your opinion too now since you no doubt take everything in this book as the Gospel truth!) While many insureds just focus on the percentage figure and assume that's what they'll be charged, underwriters should rightly point out that the percentage is a maximum ceiling and that market conditions and other factors at the time that the run-off is actually quoted may cause the carrier to offer a percentage below the cap amount. The cap provides comfort to an insured that it won't be charged anything in excess of that amount, but by using the "of not more than..." language it preserves the option for a lower-cost quote.

Many insureds aren't aware of an important fact with respect to D&O run-off insurance: As mentioned earlier, it doesn't have to be purchased from the carrier who wrote the expiring D&O policy. D&O run-off insurance, as a rule, is very profitable for carriers – after all, people with large claims don't normally wait to file them until after a company is bought or liquidated – so many insurers are willing to quote run-off coverage for a company whose expiring D&O Insurance they did not write.

Defense and Settlement

This section can be packed with a number of important provisions and bears reviewing carefully. Among other things, the Defense and Settlement Clause can address:

- *Advancement of Defense Costs* - This provision confirms that the carrier will advance defense costs for covered (or ostensibly covered) claims, <u>but</u> it also usually states how often such costs will be paid by the carrier (e.g. as incurred or only quarterly) and frequently states that amounts paid that are later deemed to have been unjustified must be repaid to the carrier – although this provision is seldom invoked. My theory is that most carriers don't want to be known within the professional lines insurance community (which is relatively small and tight-knit as opposed to other segments of insurance) as insurance companies who pursue their insureds to recover payments already made. While pursuing an insured for uncovered payments might save a carrier $2 million in recovered defense costs, it could ultimately cost $10 million in lost new business opportunities with brokers who hear about the recovery and avoid placing clients with that carrier. Also, as a practical matter, in some instances insureds simply don't have the money to repay uncovered defense costs which were erroneously advanced. As with many provisions of a standard D&O Insurance policy, what appears to be a coverage grant is actually a coverage restriction in certain ways.

- *Consent to Settle* - Requires the insured to get the carrier's consent before agreeing to settle any claim that will involve a payment under the D&O policy. Usually drafted in an expansive way, this provision also prohibits the insureds from even making a settlement offer, never mind actually settling, without the carrier's approval. It also prevents the insured from incurring defense costs or admitting any liability without the insurer's prior consent. Frequently, D&O policies will state that the insurer's consent to the above matters cannot be "unreasonably withheld," which is a phrase that's open to interpretation. When dealing with insureds who incur a high volume of claims, some carriers will agree to not contest the validity of any settlement made under a certain amount without prior approval (such as when a settlement offer requires a quick response and the carrier cannot comply that quickly) but the carrier will reserve the right to contest the reasonableness of the settlement amount paid. Generally, however, most insureds don't have a high volume of D&O claims, and this exception is used primarily on E&O policies.

- *Cooperation* - This section establishes that the insureds must cooperate with the carrier in investigating and defending all claims and shall do nothing to prejudice the insurer's rights of subrogation (if any exist). While these may seem to be basic aspects of any liability insurance policy which needn't be reduced to writing, you'd be surprised at how often the specific requirements of this section must be invoked by a carrier. Insureds sometimes don't want to reveal incriminating facts to their carrier because they feel this information may harm their company's reputation and/or result in other undesirable consequences, such as loss of insurance coverage and/or criminal prosecution. The policyholder may also fear the loss of the protection of the attorney-client privilege if they reveal certain facts to their carrier (although the joint-defense doctrine in many jurisdictions may alleviate this concern.) Cooperation Clause requirements are rarely negotiable because: a.) They are integral to a D&O policy's operation; and b.) Carriers generally don't want to insure a company that indicates from the outset that it won't fully cooperate with the carrier when a claim arises.

- *Duty to Defend* - Unlike many Errors and Omissions (E&O) insurance policies, D&O forms are almost never "duty to defend" policies, thus, the insureds bear the burden of selecting and retaining their own defense counsel – but only with the carrier's approval. The carrier will review a wide variety of factors, such as the chosen law firm's experience in defending matters of this nature, the firm's geographic location in relation to the claim's venue and, not inconsequentially, the attorneys' billing rates. Two theories as to why insurance carriers don't want to assume the duty to defend under a D&O policy are: 1) D&O suits can sometimes have a significant impact on a company's fortunes (even bankrupting them in some instances in what's known as "bet the company" litigation), and carriers don't want to risk incurring liability for selecting a law firm that performs inadequately; and 2) Many directors and senior executives wouldn't purchase a D&O Insurance policy that allows an insurance company to select legal counsel to defend the insureds in complex litigation with potentially enormous ramifications. They don't necessarily trust the carrier to select the best firm possible and with the not unreasonable belief that they know what is best for their company, they want to make the choice of counsel decision. Almost all D&O Insurance policies agree to cover only the "reasonable and necessary" defense costs of insureds in a claim. When an insurance carrier deems a law firm's hourly billing rates to be unacceptably high (i.e. "unreasonable") but the insured still wants to retain that firm, insurers will sometimes agree to allow the insured to pay the portion of the hourly rate above what the insurer normally pays (sometimes called "the overage") in exchange for the insurer's approval of the firm. Some D&O carriers maintain a list of pre-approved law firms (known as "panel counsel") that they require insureds to use for certain claims, such as securities class actions. While this practice was more prevalent in the 1990s, it seems to be losing popularity in today's market. Most insureds prefer freedom of choice when selecting defense counsel under a D&O policy no matter what the claim (although, again, carriers usually retain the right to approve or veto selected law firms.)

- *Settlement Clause (also known as the "Hammer Clause")* - This section of the policy caps the insurer's liability in the event that a claimant agrees to accept a specific amount of money to settle a claim but the insured refuses to consent to such a settlement. The reasons for an insured's unwillingness to settle vary, but among them might be the insured company's desire to prove its innocence in court to protect its reputation and/or a belief that the claimant is not entitled to such a large settlement (which could, theoretically, lead to increased D&O premiums for the insured). Carriers differ on their approach to the cap on their liability under a Settlement Clause. Some insurers, adopting the most draconian approach, declare that they will be liable for no greater payment for a claim then the amount of defense costs incurred up to the point of the claimant's agreement to specific settlement amount plus the amount of the acceptable settlement payment itself. Other carriers institute a coinsurance feature after the point of the definitive settlement is reached (and rejected by the insured), making the insured liable for a specified percentage of all loss incurred after the settlement offer is rejected. A typical Settlement Claus coinsurance penalty would be 50 percent, although the figure varies by carrier and policy and usually can be negotiated. When I was an underwriting manager, I would tell our clients that we sell liability policies and when we get to the point where the insureds' liability could be definitively extinguished, our policy has performed its intended function. From that point forward, if the insured company wants to fight to protect its reputation (or for any other reason), it has to bear all, or some meaningful percentage, of the cost. In my experience, many times when faced with this choice, insureds determine that their reputation isn't worth the risk of a much larger judgment that may exceed their insurance limits and they agree to settle (although sometimes not until they're on the courthouse steps.) I was once involved in a high-profile claim involving professional athletes which garnered national media attention. The defendants insisted on "fighting to the finish" to protect their reputation and prove that they were right. However, the day before trial was to begin, when the media attention was at its most intense and the specter of a plaintiffs' verdict loomed, the insureds demanded that the carrier kick in the remainder of the D&O policy's limit in order to settle the matter. The carrier complied and the matter settled, but for a total payout which could've been much less had the defendants agreed to earlier settlement opportunities. (It was not a total waste however; at least it gave me some additional material for this book!)

- *Settlement Within Retention* - Many D&O Insurance policies allow the insured to settle a claim within the self-insured retention amount without the carrier's prior approval, which would seem to make sense since the carrier is not paying anything toward the settlement. The caveat here, one that's important, is that the settlement must address all aspects of such claim(s) and cannot leave anything open. Obviously, the carrier wouldn't want the insured to consummate a partial settlement without its approval, which then leaves open potential larger claims that could be strengthened by the terms of the partial settlement, especially if the insured stipulated to any unfavorable facts.

Estates, Spouses, Legal Representatives

Theoretically, although it rarely happens, people legally connected to insureds under a D&O policy can lose their assets if marital or other jointly held property (or bequeathed property in the event that the insured has died) were to be attacked in a claim. D&O carriers broadened their policies many years ago to provide coverage to spouses and then, over time, that extension was liberalized to include domestic partners (usually only in jurisdictions where they are legally recognized as such), heirs, legal representatives and assigns. It's important to note, however, that these additional classes of people are not insured for their own independent acts, errors and omissions; they only receive coverage to the extent that liability attaches to them by virtue of their connection to an insured under the policy. This makes perfect sense, of course, since the legally-connected parties are not directly affiliated with the insured company and really shouldn't receive coverage for their own acts.

This is one of the aspects of D&O Insurance that promotes better sleep for those connected to insureds, although, again, it is rarely called on to respond to a claim.

Extended Reporting Period

Also known as the Discovery Period, the Extended Reporting Period (frequently referred to simply as the ERP), is an additional period of time afforded to insureds to report a claim after the policy's expiration – either through natural expiration or cancellation. The ERP typically runs for one year, but it's not unusual for an insured to negotiate a three-year, and in some cases even as long as a six-year, ERP. It's important to note that carriers generally will only accept notice of a claim during the ERP if the claim arises from wrongful acts committed before the policy's expiration. Thus, the ERP does not apply to claims arising from wrongful acts committed after the policy's expiration (if it did, then the policy would not technically be expired).

Insureds usually only have a short window of time to elect the ERP after the policy's termination. Ten days seems to be the norm, although it can also be elected in advance of the actual termination date. Carriers almost universally require the notice of election to be in writing and, also, they require the payment of an additional premium within a very short time frame (also usually ten days). This additional premium for the ERP is normally calculated as a percentage of the policy's annual premium and is often pre-set and stated on the policy form at inception. By way of example, a one-year ERP may cost 150 percent of the policy's full annual premium, and a three-year ERP may cost 200 percent of the full annual premium. These are only examples, and actual numbers vary depending upon a variety of factors, including the insured's claims history, financial condition and the state of the D&O Insurance market. In soft markets ERPs are cheaper than in a firm market.

In earlier years, insurers made the ERP a unilateral proposition, that is, an insured could only elect the ERP if the insurer canceled or non-renewed the D&O policy. Eventually, the concept of "bilateral discovery" was created. This occurred during a soft-market period, which is when coverage terms tend to broaden. It seems to this self-described astute observer that when rates sink to a level that carriers deem are the minimum actuarially-approved rate per million, they switch from competing on lower prices to competing on liberalized coverage. Not a good recipe for the bottom lines of carriers, but, nonetheless, it happens.

Bilateral discovery allows the insured to elect the ERP even when the insured itself cancels or non-renews the policy, which is a significant enhancement to the rights of an insured under a D&O policy in comparison to unilateral discovery.

Almost all carriers state that a change in the terms, conditions, premium and retention on the renewal quote does not constitute a non-renewal that would trigger an ERP election opportunity. This language is superfluous in a bilateral discovery policy however, since even if the carrier doesn't non-renew, the insured could simply decline the renewal quote and declare that it is non-renewing the policy of its own volition.

It's important to note that the standard ERP only provides additional time to report claims under the policy's pre-existing limit of liability – they don't create a new stand-alone limit of liability. Thus, if the expiring policy's limit had been depleted, say from $10 million down to $7 million, if the insured were to elect the ERP only $7 million would be available to respond to claims first made during the Extended Reporting Period. However, it is possible, on a case-by-case basis, to purchase a new limit of liability to apply to the ERP. Many times (although not necessarily always) this would be in a "run-off" situation where the insured company is being acquired, merged, liquidated or is otherwise ceasing to exist in its previous form.

Generally speaking, most carriers view ERP premium as gravy. It seems that when a potential claimant has a significant claim, they do not wait an extended period before attempting to enforce their rights. This is especially true when a company is going out of business or being acquired – potential plaintiffs hear the news and file their claim fairly quickly in most instances. Some insureds, exercising an abundance of caution, purchase six-year ERPs because the statute of limitations for some civil wrongs is six years. However, if you were to poll claims professionals, you'd find that very few claims are ever reported in years four, five or six of a six-year ERP. If you have a major claim against a company, most likely you're not going to wait an extended period of time before making it.

It's also important to point out that an insured doesn't necessarily have to purchase their ERP from the carrier who provided the original coverage. Depending upon specific circumstances, many carriers are more than happy to quote an ERP, or "run-off" on another carrier's account because, again, they are seeking to collect the "gravy" premium frequently associated with an ERP.

Limits of Liability

This section of a D&O policy usually establishes that defense costs are part of the overall limit of liability and they deplete the limit as they are paid. Policies with this feature are sometimes referred to as "self-liquidating," "self-wasting" or simply "wasting" policies. While exact wording and intent varies from carrier to carrier, this section can also set forth the concept of interrelated wrongful acts. This normally states that the date of the first claim arising from such interrelated wrongful act shall be considered the date of origin for all claims arising from such interrelated wrongful acts. This is an important detail because it may result in the claim being classified as being first made before the policy period began, thereby removing it from eligibility for coverage.

Some D&O policies, typically only those that cover non-profit or private companies, contain a "defense outside the limits" feature which does not result in defense costs depleting the policy's limit of liability. However, these policies usually contain a feature that will allow the carrier to cap its payment of defense costs at some point, such as when the amount of defense costs equals the policy's total limit of liability (or some other number).

In some situations, such as when an applicant company is particularly troubled (thereby making the carrier uncomfortable) or when the applicant can't afford (or doesn't want to pay for) full coverage, a "defense only" policy may be written. This type of policy provides a limit of liability that only pays defense costs associated with covered claims; it doesn't apply to settlements or judgments. While not "Option A" for most companies seeking D&O coverage, a defense only policy can sometimes provide vital protection at a more affordable cost.

Other Insurance

Almost all D&O policies contain a provision stating that they apply only as "excess over any other valid and collectible insurance" with an exception for other insurance that is "specifically written as excess over this policy." Some carriers, but not all, say that in order for such other insurance to be classified as excess of their policy, it must specifically reference the carrier's underlying policy by number.

Sometimes, when more than one policy applies to a claim, a situation may occur that is known as "dueling other insurance clauses." This may happen when two D&O policies apply to the same insureds for the same claim or when different types of policies, a D&O and an E&O for example, apply to a single claim. One method of resolving this dispute is to simply have each policy pay a per capita share of the total loss (e.g. if there are two policies, each pays half; if there are three, each pays a third). Another solution is to have each policy pay a share of the loss according to its proportion of the total limits applicable to the claim. So, for example, if one carrier wrote a $5 million policy and another wrote a $10 million policy, each applicable to the same claim, an argument could be made that the $10 million policy's carrier signed on for a bigger risk and should therefore pay two-thirds of all loss since $10 million is two-thirds of the total $15 million limit available to the insured.

Other Insurance clauses sometimes contain what's known as a "non-stacking" or "non-pyramiding" feature. This provision states that if the carrier (or any of its affiliated/sister companies) writes more than one policy that applies to a single claim, any payment under one of the policies shall reduce the applicable limit of liability for that claim under the other policy. In today's market, this is normally only applicable to an outside directorship situation where the director of Company A also sits on the board of Company B and each company has a D&O Insurance policy that applies to the same claim. In earlier days of D&O Insurance, non-stacking provisions weren't limited to just outside directorship situations; they were much broader and would apply to any situation involving two or more policies written under the same parent-company umbrella, regardless of the type of policy or claim involved. Many people, however, felt that blanket non-stacking clauses were unfair given that the various policies involved were underwritten separately and insureds paid separate (and presumably adequate) premiums for each.

Priority of Payments

This concept originated in the mid-1990s and is intended to establish, in advance of needing such guidance, the order in which the D&O policy's proceeds are paid when multiple insureds are defendants in one or more claims. Usually, the Priority of Payments clause states that individual insureds will receive first priority in getting their loss paid under Side A of the D&O policy, next comes Side B loss and then Side C losses are paid (note: outside directorship liability (ODL) claims, if coverage for them is provided, usually takes preference over Side C claim payments), but this is by no means written in stone. Some Priority of Payments clauses state that the CEO of the insured entity (or some other specifically-designated individual, such as the insured's president or managing general partner, if applicable) can request that the insurer delay or withhold payments until his or her authorization is provided. This provision would be relevant when, for example, the insured defendants have a disagreement over who deserves coverage under the D&O

policy (such as in a situation where one or more insureds are accused of fraud, self-dealing or other egregious conduct) and the CEO or another designated individual wants additional time to sort out things before requesting payment from the carrier. Insurers also favor this approach because otherwise they can be caught in the unenviable position of having to decide the order of priority of paying loss among the competing factions of insureds, which could potentially create liability for the insurer. This provision can be tailored in many ways, and while most insureds do not give it much thought when purchasing a D&O policy, ultimately the priority of payments provision can end up being one of the policy's most critical features.

Retentions

The retention is the amount of risk that the insured retains for itself. Some carriers use this section of the D&O policy to establish that no retention applies to non-indemnifiable loss and, in some cases, other types of loss for additional coverage granted (such as for the cost of investigations into derivative demands when such coverage is provided). This is also the section where normally insurers state that only a single retention will apply to all loss arising from interrelated claims.

Confusion can arise, especially among newer participants in the commercial insurance industry, over the difference between a retention (also referred to as a "self-insured retention" or "SIR" for short) and a deductible. While definitions may vary from policy to policy and insurer to insurer, generally, as mentioned above, a retention refers to the portion of an insured loss that is <u>retained</u> by the insured and, thus, the insured must pay this amount before the insurer will provide coverage. Many otherwise insured losses are disposed of for payments that are wholly within the self-insured retention amount and, thus, the carrier is not required to pay anything on those claims.

A "deductible," a term familiar to many insureds from their auto or homeowners' insurance, is generally an amount of money that an insurer deducts from its claim payment when made. Thus, the insured doesn't have to come out of pocket initially to satisfy the deductible amount before coverage applies (unlike with a self-insured retention) but, rather, the carrier makes payment from the first dollar of loss and then subtracts the amount of the deductible from the check sent to the insured. By way of example, assume an insured backs his car into a tree and incurs $2,000 worth of damage to his vehicle. If he has a $500 deductible on his auto insurance policy, the insurer would send the insured a check for $1,500. If that $500 were termed a retention instead of a deductible, the insured would be required to pay the auto body shop the first $500 before the insurer would pay the remaining $1,500. But, again, to be clear, most personal lines insurance policies use deductibles, not retentions. Also, depending upon the specific policy in question, the deductible amount may reduce the policy's limit of liability in some instances.

It's worth noting that in some policies, such as those that cover Cyber Liability or systems breakdowns for financial institutions, the SIR may be expressed as a period of time, such as 24 hours or three days. In these cases, the policy's coverage doesn't begin until an insured system or function has been inoperative for the specified period of time.

Subrogation

The subrogation clauses of various D&O Insurance policies can vary in substantial respects, although most share the same basic provisions. Generally, they will all state that in the event of a payment under the policy, the insurer is subrogated to the rights of recovery of the insureds. They also establish that the insureds agree to execute any papers and provide any assistance and cooperation necessary for the carrier to exercise its right of subrogation. There are two important areas where they can differ, however.

First, many subrogation clauses are silent on the issue of pursuing subrogation against an insured. Some specifically state that the carrier can pursue payment from the corporate entity insured for losses paid on behalf of an individual insured. When the policy is silent on this issue, however, it's implied that the insurer can pursue an individual insured for subrogation with respect to losses that the carrier believes it wrongfully paid on the individual's behalf. Most insureds and brokers are not comfortable with that concept, yet if the issue isn't explicitly raised, it often goes unaddressed.

Some policies state that the carrier will only pursue subrogation against an individual insured if a specific conduct exclusion applies to previously paid loss (e.g. the insured was adjudicated to be guilty of fraud and now the carrier wants its defense cost payments back). In reality, carriers almost never assert subrogation rights to pursue individual insureds for payments previously made. In my 20-plus years in the insurance industry, I may have seen it happen two or three times, if that. There are a number of reasons as to why carriers don't pursue individual insureds for subrogation. Among them: 1) No carrier wants the adverse publicity in the marketplace of being known as a company that will pursue its own insureds for payment – especially at a time when the insured has suffered through a claim and is expecting the carrier to provide protection, not prosecution; 2) Most defendants who've been convicted of fraud are left with few personal assets (or have gone to the trouble of hiding them), and it's just not worth the carrier's time and effort to pursue payment; and 3) Insurers like to close files, collect reinsurance and move on; following up on subrogation claims against individual insureds can take many years and prolong the file-closing and reinsurance collections process considerably.

The second significant area where subrogation clauses can differ involves the order of repayment. It should be noted, however, that the successful execution of a subrogation claim by insurers in general – against any party – not just against insureds, is a rare occurrence in the D&O Insurance world. Nonetheless, in those few instances when it does occur, it's nice to have the order of repayment spelled out clearly in the D&O policy. Generally, carriers favor a reverse chronological order of repayment. Thus, the first payment of loss made, the insured's self-insured retention, would be the first repaid from any funds recovered through subrogation. Next, the portion of loss insured and paid under the policy would be repaid to the carrier. And, finally, any excess over the policy's limits paid by the insured would be repaid. In reality, the insured's odds of receiving repayment through subrogation for amounts it paid in excess of policy limits to resolve a claim are about the same as its odds of being hit by Haley's Comet. But, still, one can hope. Some carriers will attempt to recover their costs of pursuing the subrogation claim (i.e., their lawyer's fees and any court costs) before any other repayments are made. Unless it's specifically stated in the policy (or endorsements), the order of repayment is generally subject to negotiation. But, again, recovering under the subrogation clause is so rare that only a very scholarly and in-depth book such as this would even bother mentioning it!

Territory

Most policies today cover claims arising from wrongful acts that occur worldwide (including in cyberspace), although the policy (especially if issued by a U.S.-based carrier) may require that the claim itself be brought in the United States and some other specified jurisdictions to be eligible for coverage. Some policies also state that claims will only be paid in U.S. dollars based on an exchange rate appearing in the

Wall Street Journal on the date that the claim is settled or adjudicated. In one sense, it appears fair that U.S.-based carriers require claims to be brought in the United States or a short list of other nations with a similar legal system because it would be difficult to underwrite a policy properly based on claims that may arise in some distant country under unknown laws that may change regularly. But, on the other hand, more and more companies are doing business internationally – especially because of the internet – and the commercial insurance-buying community's need for truly international coverage has never been greater. If necessary, a longer list of acceptable countries can sometimes be included for coverage once the request has been made and the carrier has had an opportunity to underwrite each country's legal system and claims climate individually (as well as the extent of the insured's activities in such foreign jurisdictions).

Some carriers exclude coverage (usually by endorsement) for claims arising in specific countries where there is civil unrest and/or a revolutionary or temporary government in control. One reason for this is that a carrier doesn't want to pay a claim today under that nation's current legal system and then have a new government take power tomorrow and declare that the previous claim payment is unrecognized under the new system of laws and must be paid again.

Understanding Specific Risks

Underwriting D&O Insurance, as you probably know, especially this far into the book, is not a one-size-fits-all proposition. For example, an insurance professional who understands the significance of every clause in a standard D&O Insurance policy and is an outstanding underwriter of non-profit organizations may be totally lost when it comes to underwriting a bank. Or a gaming company. Or a biotech firm. Specific knowledge of individual companies and their industries is critical to properly underwriting D&O Insurance.

This is not to say, however, that D&O Insurance cannot be responsibly underwritten on a high-volume program basis with minimal individual risk analysis. In fact, it's quite possible to do so when dealing with fairly uncomplicated accounts (sometimes called "cookie cutter" business) that only require low limits and standardized coverages without many, if any, modifications to the basic D&O policy form. In such an instance, carriers are said to be underwriting a "class of business" as a whole, without as much concern for individual account metrics. For example, an insurer might decide that community banks based in Iowa and Minnesota with less than $900 million in total assets are all good D&O Insurance risks. That carrier might, therefore, develop a "black-box" underwriting plan for such accounts. This black-box underwriting scheme would not require individual risk analysis except in special circumstances, such as, for example, if the bank had a paid D&O claim in the previous five years. Or if the asset size changed by more than 20 percent in the previous year. Those applicants with special risk factors such as these would be "referred" (or "kicked out") to an underwriter who would then individually review that bank's application (assuming, of course, that nothing in the applicant's risk profile totally excluded the company right from the start.)

Having said that, most midsize – and certainly all larger – D&O accounts will require some level of individualized review and underwriting. Below are general guidelines to keep in mind during this process.

A. Reviewing the Applicant's Risk Profile

There's an often-repeated saying in the investment business: "Past performance is no guarantee of future results." While this is also true in the insurance world, past performance can provide valuable insights into an applicant company and must be considered in order to thoroughly underwrite an account.

Most, if not all, D&O Insurance carriers use what's known as an underwriting worksheet in an attempt to capture a number of significant metrics and other information relating to an applicant company's risk profile. The key word here is "attempt" because no underwriting worksheet is perfect and too much blind reliance on an underwriting worksheet can prove disastrous. But, make no mistake, there is at least *some value* to an underwriting worksheet, especially as a starting point for further investigation.

Years ago, when I was at AIG, an underwriter came into my office to review a Securities Broker/Dealer E&O account that was about to renew. We went through the basic metrics and significant factors that were recorded on the underwriting worksheet and everything seemed to be in order. The worksheet attempted to assign a risk value to the mix of investment products sold by the broker/dealer firm, although it was an inexact science at best. For example, a firm that sold a lot of limited partnership shares would be considered riskier than one that mostly sold mutual funds.

Just before he left my office, I asked the underwriter "Is there anything else that I should know about this account? Anything new happening?

"Well, yeah, one thing I guess," he replied, "The firm listed a new investment product that they're now selling. They're called viatical settlements. I'm not really sure what that means."

This was in the early days of viatical settlements, which were arrangements whereby companies paid upfront money to terminally-ill holders of life insurance policies in exchange for being named the beneficiary of such policies. These settlements were sometimes securitized and sold to the public. Neither of us knew what they were at the time. Fortunately, we did some further research and, also, we questioned the company directly about how this investment product would work. Ultimately, we ended up excluding viatical settlement claims from coverage. It turned out to be a wise move because quite a few claims arose from that investment product over the next few years. Had we just accepted the disclosure as it was without additional investigation, we would've had significant losses on our hands. Even though this was an E&O account, the example applies equally to D&O Insurance.

An underwriting worksheet can be a valuable tool but is not the be-all/end-all when it comes to assessing risk. It's important, in my opinion, to take a holistic approach when underwriting accounts that merit individual consideration, as opposed to small "cookie cutter" program business. A holistic approach entails reviewing a wide range of factors, including off-the-grid considerations that may not be captured by standard risk-assessment tools.

1. Assessing the Application

Most insurers use a very broad definition of the term "Application" (see above). It no longer consists of simply a written application form in the traditional sense, as it did in earlier days of D&O Insurance.

Today, an application can also include public filings with government entities – whether or not they're specifically submitted with, or referenced in, the application form itself – as well as various other pieces of information, such as news releases and other public statements. All of these materials are usually easily obtainable on the internet. The "Information Superhighway" makes it difficult for a D&O

applicant, especially one that's publicly traded, to successfully conceal significant information – unless, of course, fraud is involved. (*"No, of course not, Mr. Madoff, we're not accusing you of anything. We'd just like you to provide financials with your application."[6]*)

When one uses a holistic approach to analyze an applicant's risk profile, it becomes apparent that, in most cases, no single factor will determine whether a risk is acceptable or not. Rather, an assessment must be made only after viewing the applicant's entire risk profile as a whole. There are exceptions to this rule, of course, but even seemingly insurmountable negative developments at an applicant company, such as an imminent bankruptcy filing or a recent senior management shake-up, can many times be analyzed and "underwritten to" so the carrier can craft a policy that's both acceptable to the insured and within the carrier's risk tolerance.

---

[6] Tangential story: When I was at Professional Indemnity Agency, Inc., an underwriting subsidiary of Houston Casualty, we received a submission to quote Bernard Madoff's fidelity bond coverage. Our senior fidelity underwriter, George Blume, didn't like the risk for a number of reasons, including the fact that one man, Mr. Madoff, had complete authority to disburse company funds without any oversight. Best practices in fidelity underwriting dictate that at least two people must approve (or "sign off on") all financial transactions over a certain amount. This, in theory anyway, decreases the likelihood of embezzlement because it would require two criminals working in concert to carry out the fraudulent activity. Luckily for HCC, George declined the submission. There wasn't necessarily one determining factor underlying George's position, but overall he just didn't get a good feeling about the account. This is further proof that sometimes an underwriter's gut feeling can save the day.

Most application forms today have been streamlined compared to days gone by, when the typical application contained page after page of questions. My guess is that this "skinnying down" of the application form is due to two main factors: 1) The market has become very competitive and most brokers and insureds prefer to do business with user-friendly carriers who don't burden them with a lot of information requests; and 2) There is so much information available on the internet these days that an underwriter only needs a few basic facts before setting off on a search to get a much better picture of the applicant. Despite all the information available on the internet, however, an application is always the best place to start an analysis of a D&O Insurance risk. The application can provide a general overview of a company's current status while also pointing an underwriter in the right direction to gather additional information.

Today's streamlined applications usually ask a number of generic questions. Besides the most obvious (e.g. name of company, state of incorporation, nature of business, current D&O Insurance limits, D&O claims history, etc.), applications will ask things such as whether the company is publicly traded and, if so, on what exchange(s) and what subsidiaries the applicant may own. Just about every new-line application (i.e. the initial application for insurance with a carrier new to the program) also contains a warranty statement of some type wherein individual insureds affirm (as a group) that they are aware of no circumstances that are reasonably likely to give rise to a claim under the proposed insurance coverage. The vast majority of claims-made insurance policy renewal applications do not contain a warranty statement because if the insureds know of anything reasonably likely to give rise to a claim (or, as some applications state, "which might give rise to a claim"), normally the insureds can just report it under the expiring policy as a Notice of Potential Claim.

Beyond the basic application information, here are some things that a thorough underwriter should review and consider.

2. Performing Deeper Research

Analyst Reports

Analyst reports and ratings only apply to companies that are publicly traded, thus they're not a universal D&O Insurance underwriting tool. However, when dealing with publicly-traded companies, analyst ratings and reports can be helpful, especially when viewed in the aggregate. Most stock analysts only follow a limited number of companies in specific industry niches. This allows them to devote far more time to in-depth research on a company than could an underwriter who may receive numerous submissions a day and is under great pressure to underwrite the applicants quickly to generate quotes (and premium revenue). Also, analysts almost always have the opportunity to meet with the senior management team of companies they're covering to conduct detailed discussions. Underwriters sometimes get this opportunity, but certainly not always. Thus, for these reasons and others, analysts can often uncover important information that might otherwise escape an underwriter's notice.

Analyst ratings are most useful when viewed collectively. Are the majority of analysts saying that the company's stock should be sold? Or are most of the analysts bullish on the company and anointing it with their highest ratings? It's also important to pay attention to trends. Over the past six to 12 months have analysts been upgrading or downgrading their opinion of the stock? If the trend is toward downgrades, that could signal that something is wrong at the company. In that case, underwriters would be wise to remember an adage from the investment world: *"Never catch a falling knife."*[7] An underwriter who takes a chance on providing D&O Insurance to a company whose share price and ratings are falling may well get injured by the blade of the falling knife. Of course, this is a general statement and individual circumstances may merit writing an account on the downswing in certain situations, for example, when there is convincing proof that a blockbuster new product introduction is close at hand.

Financial Press

To be sure, the financial press can, at times, be manipulated by a company through the use of high-powered public relations firms and other methods to produce rosy

---

[7] D&O Insurance underwriters are wise to heed principles of investing because, after all, by issuing a D&O Insurance they are investing their employer's capital in support of the insured company and its management.

articles about the company's performance and prospects. But for the most part, especially when reviewing a large sampling, the financial press provides valuable insights into a company's current status and future direction. One of the keys to using the financial press as an underwriting tool is to know which sources should be trusted and which might have inherent prejudices (such as industry-sponsored periodicals) and which can be manipulated to provide a slanted view.

Company research through the media shouldn't just be limited to the financial press however; valuable insights can be gleaned from mainstream, non-financial media as well. Significant issues, such as product liability lawsuits, impending layoffs, store closings and senior management scandals, just to name a few, are often covered in the mainstream media and sometimes with great insight. When it comes to reviewing media reports and publicly available information, nothing should be off-limits; however, one must consider the credibility and impartialness of each source.

Specific Performance Metrics (EPS, BETA, etc.)

Specific performance metrics, like many factors to be considered during the D&O Insurance underwriting process, should be viewed from both a trend perspective within the history of the individual applicant company as well as in comparison to other companies in the applicant's overall industry niche.

For example, it doesn't do much good to know that a company's earnings per share (EPS[8]) equates to $5 if that's all you know with respect to that particular company and its EPS. In order to maximize the analytical value of the EPS figure, you'd need to compare the current EPS with the company's historic EPS numbers over the past three to five years (generally, the longer the period of comparison, the better). By doing this, you'd be able to determine what trends are emerging, such as whether the company is becoming more, or less, profitable over time. To hammer home an important concept set forth above: Underwriters should always attempt to identify various trends with respect to any applicant company. Although the old saying tells us, as noted previously, that "Past performance is not a guarantee of future results," recent past performance, especially when indicative of specific trends, may provide valuable guidance as to what the future may hold.

It's also important to compare trends of specific metrics within particular industry niches to see how an applicant company stacks up against its competition. It's not good enough to compare, say, the EPS of a manufacturer of flat-screen TVs to the EPS of a maker of smartphones on the theory that they are both makers of electronic devices. Rather, they should each be compared to companies within their specific niche of electronics. And, of course, that industry niche should be compared to overall industry averages and even the

---

[8] Without getting too technical, EPS is calculated by subtracting a company's preferred stock dividend payments from net income over a given period of time and then dividing the total by the average number of outstanding shares of company stock during that time period.

larger marketplace as a whole. If one particular niche or industry is performing poorly during an otherwise booming economy, it could be a signal that all companies within that grouping should be avoided by underwriters. Similarly, an above-average performer in a downtrodden industry niche does not necessarily make for a good D&O Insurance risk. For instance, assuming that there were multiple manufacturers of audio cassette tapes still in business (and this were their sole product line), no competent underwriter would believe that the most successful of such companies would be a good long-term D&O Insurance risk.

3. The Art of Underwriting with Intangibles

Firsthand Knowledge

Firsthand knowledge is an interesting underwriting tool. I use the term "firsthand knowledge" not to refer to research that you've reviewed first hand, but rather knowledge that you as an underwriter have come across while dealing with the applicant company in question. For example, if you're underwriting a retail clothing chain and you notice that every time you patronize one of its locations the store has few customers and is stocked with nothing but out-of-fashion clothing, then this would constitute a valuable firsthand insight. You can read all of the analyst reports you'd like, but there's nothing quite so powerful, and telling, as looking at a store devoid of customers on what should otherwise be a busy Saturday afternoon. Merchandise that isn't in fashion, a uniformly surly and uncooperative attitude among the salespeople (possibly caused by poor working conditions and/or compensation) and similar factors could also be clues that the company doesn't have a rosy future.

Of course, as with other pieces of information, you need to view firsthand knowledge in the proper light. Were weather conditions poor and thus discouraging people from shopping on the particular days you visited the stores? Were your visits on long weekends when people were away on holiday retreats? Did a competing retailer have a grand opening down the road on one of those days, thus siphoning off customers who would otherwise be present? Firsthand knowledge should be applied through the prism of a holistic approach, just like almost all other underwriting indicators, so that you can view it in a greater context to determine where this information fits in the overall scheme of things. In the example above, it would be wise to visit not just one store but at least a few if you were really going to use firsthand knowledge in your underwriting. One "big box" national retailer who I used to underwrite had a policy that required all board members to visit a different store location each month to inspect operations and get a feel for how the business was doing. To me, that's further proof that firsthand knowledge can be valuable. Certainly, the vast majority of accounts that come across an underwriter's desk will not present an opportunity for firsthand knowledge. For example, you wouldn't randomly start ingesting prescription drugs manufactured by a pharmaceutical company applicant – but when you can prudently apply your own firsthand knowledge to the analysis of an account, it's usually beneficial.

When I was at AIG we were presented with a submission from a well-known discount broker/dealer firm seeking both D&O Insurance and E&O coverage. Let's call it ABC Brokerage. I had used a couple of other discount broker/dealer firms for my personal account before settling on ABC Brokerage, so I had a bit of firsthand knowledge in the field. In my opinion, as a client, ABC Brokerage was head-and-shoulders above the competition, a fact that was only reinforced for me during the underwriting process. We wrote the account for many years at both AIG and ACE and it continued to be a profitable piece of business during the entire time I was involved. The firsthand knowledge I had was not the sole driver in our underwriting decisions, but it certainly helped. I was confident that ABC Brokerage provided superior products and services to its clients and the company's long-term performance was in sync with my analysis.

Internet Banter

The internet provides plenty of opportunities to gather intelligence on companies and individuals. Of course, not all of it is accurate, despite what some people may think. *"Don't believe everything you read,"* is truer today than ever because of the internet. At least most newspapers – although they seem to be heading toward extinction – use editors and other fact-checkers as something of a safeguard against misinformation. Message boards, blogs, e-zines, chat rooms and other internet-based sources of "information" often have no such precautionary measures in place. One person, as most of us know, can make up their own "facts" and spread them like a wildfire on the World Wide Web. Still, an underwriter can be well served by considering internet banter in the proper light.

Message boards – sites where people can exchange ideas freely on various topics, including a company, its stock price and future prospects – can, believe it or not, sometimes offer worthwhile insights. The trick is knowing how to sift through a lot of pap in order to extract the few nuggets of golden information. Anyone who has ever read a message board knows that they can contain a lot of personal attacks and wholly irrelevant ads for products and services. *However*, occasionally an important issue or fact may surface which, if researched further using more reliable sources, may yield valuable information. To some extent, a person must use their intuition to figure out which leads are worth following on a message board, but some rules of thumb do apply. For example, if multiple people are making similar claims on the message board, it may be a sign that there's some truth to what they're saying. Also, if a poster (that is, a person who posts a message) has established a track record of posting predictions that come true – which can be verified easily enough by checking the message board's historical postings – it may be a sign that she or he has some type of insider knowledge (although not necessarily insider knowledge that is illegal to disclose, maybe just the common complaints of an average employee of the company).

The takeaway here is that while message boards and the like are certainly not rock-solid sources of information upon which an underwriter can definitively rely, they can, nonetheless, be a source of additional intelligence on a company and/or its directors and officers and should not be cavalierly dismissed as merely the rantings of an ill-informed public. Used properly, they can be a useful underwriting tool.

It's also important to keep in mind the adage *"Perception can become reality."* If enough people consistently carp about a company's management on the internet, declaring it inept when the opposite is true, a movement may nonetheless take hold to replace that management team simply because popular sentiment becomes overwhelming. Or perhaps an army of consumers have taken to the internet to complain about a company's flagship product or the quality of its service. Unified sentiments like these among a company's customer base can easily spell future trouble. An underwriter would be foolish to totally discount these scenarios in the risk-assessment process.

In-Person Visits

In these days of omnipresent conference calls, webinars, videoconferencing, emailing and other surrogates for face-to-face meetings, it seems as if the underwriting process has become less personal than it used to be, which, in my opinion, is a shame. There are many benefits to in-person visits, not the least of which is, as a wise, old insurance veteran told me early in my career, "It's a lot harder to tell someone to screw off over the phone after you've met them in person." Of course, none of us conducts our business in such a way that we expect people to tell us to "screw off" with any regularity, however, you get the point.

In-person underwriting visits can create a win/win for the insured and insurer. For example, insureds may be able to influence the carrier to provide more favorable underwriting terms and conditions than the carrier might otherwise offer to faceless applicants. On the other hand, underwriters can often glean valuable insights from insureds that would not be evident from merely reading an application and accompanying submission materials.

Below are just two real-world examples of the benefits of in-person meetings – although I could probably fill an entire book on this topic.

The first occurred when the carrier I was working for was presented with the D&O submission for a regional chain of discount consumer-goods stores which we'll call XYX Stores. (No, not Costco, so please stop guessing.) The paradigm for consumer-goods stores has to be, without question, Wal-Mart. It's the largest and most profitable such chain in American history (and probably world history as well.)

One of Wal-Mart's driving principles, as anyone knows who has ever dealt with the company from a supplier's perspective, is to maintain a low-overhead cost structure so it can pass the savings on to customers. I've never been to the company's headquarters in Bentonville, Arkansas, but I know people who have. They say that everything there is as Spartan as can be. You won't find any fancy mahogany desks, plush carpets or high-priced artwork; rather, it's all as basic and as low cost as possible.

With Wal-Mart in mind as the ideal model for a successful retail chain, I set off to visit XYZ Stores' corporate headquarters.

The building itself was quite unremarkable and, in fact, we initially drove past it as it stood, somewhat obscured, off to the side of a bustling thoroughfare in a suburb of a major East Coast city. When we circled back and found the entrance to the headquarters, I was shocked at the unassuming nature of XYZ's headquarters, especially considering that the company was quite successful and growing at a significant rate. It wasn't a true rival to Wal-Mart and Sam's Club (not many companies are), but it was certainly on their radar screen. What really took me aback was that the main entrance was unmanned by security or any other attendant (this was pre-9/11 of course) and there was a wet snow shovel leaning against the wall of the foyer just inside the front door. Talk about humble surroundings!

I felt like I was visiting the back offices of the local Five-and-Dime. (Many of you are too young to get that reference but, trust me, it works.) This hammered home for me the fact that XYZ Stores' management was not wasting resources on corporate amenities. Of course, I'm not sure if XYZ's home-office employees shared my belief that this penury was beneficial, but as a D&O Insurance underwriter, I loved it. This message of austerity in management continued to be

138

reinforced when the risk manager met us at the door and took us back to his modest cubicle from which he ran a department that pumped many millions of dollars of premium annually into the commercial insurance market.

Needless to say, this visit enhanced my impression of XYZ Stores and, coupled with other underwriting information, convinced us to offer an attractive D&O Insurance quote that eventually won the business. And, as you might guess since I'm telling this story publicly, it turned out to be profitable business for my employer over the long run.

On the other hand, in-person visits can also reveal less-than-positive information about a company.

A story which comes to mind involved an AIG underwriter who went to visit a securities brokerage firm for which AIG was writing both the D&O and E&O coverages. Obviously, systems are very important to a brokerage firm and frequent or prolonged glitches can cause both D&O and E&O losses. The underwriter met with the risk manager in the risk manager's office to review a number of issues relevant to the upcoming renewals. At the conclusion of the meeting, the risk manager offered to take the underwriter on a tour of the firm's offices, hoping to impress him. Only a few seconds after the two walked onto the firm's trading floor, a distraught trader pounded her desk and stood up and yelled "The damn system is down again, second time this week!" The risk manager stuttered a bit about it being a rare occurrence and quickly ushered the underwriter out of the area. As I recall, we significantly raised the retentions on that account. Again, that was information that you wouldn't get without a personal visit.

4. Reviewing the Applicant's History

I know I mentioned this point earlier, but it's relevant here and worth repeating: "Past performance is no guarantee of future results." With respect to investments, obviously, that means that just because a particular investment increased in value over some time in the past, there's no assurance it will continue to do so in the future. Generally, this is also true of losses when it comes to the world of D&O Insurance; just because a company has had one or more D&O claims in the past, there's no guarantee it will have more claims in the future. And, of course, a lack of D&O claims in the past also doesn't guarantee there won't be any D&O claims in the future.

However, having said all of that, a company that's had a lot of D&O claims in the past may well be plagued by chronic problems such as inferior management, poor corporate governance, subpar products and services and/or any of a number of other problems. Generally, a company with a troubled claims history is going to be a more difficult account to underwrite and probably poses greater risks to the carrier going forward than a company with a clean claims history. Another old saying: "He who ignores the past is doomed to repeat it."

Underwriters need to examine an applicant's claims history closely during the underwriting process. This rule applies to new and renewal submissions, but especially to new submissions from companies with which the underwriter may not be familiar. There are a number of specific issues that an underwriter needs to focus upon when reviewing an applicant's claims history.

Continuity of Carrier Relationships

An important factor that many underwriters overlook is an applicant company's history of insurance carrier relationships.

Insurance carriers, the realistic ones anyway, don't expect to have a perfect underwriting track record; a fair number of their insureds are going to have claims. The way that a carrier builds a profitable book of business in the long term is by maintaining a strong relationship with its insureds, including paying legitimate claims in a timely manner and providing superior customer service all around (which includes prompt and accurate policy issuance). After all, if a carrier alienates every insured after a claim is filed by, for example, unfairly declining coverage or dragging its feet to prolong payments that are due, it will lose those insureds (and their premiums) in short order. It will also earn that carrier a negative reputation which, in the relatively close-knit world of professional lines insurance, gets around quickly. Therefore, it behooves a carrier, and the insured, to maintain a long-term relationship in which the carrier can smooth out the dent in its bottom line caused by claim payments with future premiums and the insured can enjoy long-term protection from a carrier it trusts and which knows its business well.. Also, an insured who jumps around from carrier to carrier on a regular basis in pursuit of lower premiums quickly earns a reputation as a price buyer who doesn't value relationships, something which will eventually place the company in a negative light when shopping for insurance.

Unlike some other lines, D&O Insurance does not always involve a cut-and-dried claim scenario. There are often gray areas, involving questions of intent, prior knowledge and other factors that may affect coverage determinations. Under an auto policy, for example, a demolished bumper costs X amount of dollars to replace and there's not much room for discretion in the carrier's coverage decision. Or, under a life insurance policy either the person is deceased or not. But with D&O Insurance, there can be many subtle nuances that might affect the ultimate coverage decision in major ways. When a claim involves a gray area, insureds want the carrier to have every incentive to give them the benefit of the doubt. One of the main ways to do this is for the insured to maintain a long-term relationship with the carrier so that it has built up a "goodwill bank" with the carrier in the event of a claim.

Insureds who change carriers frequently don't understand this concept nor do many of them value long-term business relationships. In fact, some companies openly admit that they don't care a whit about "relationships," they just jump from carrier to carrier each year based on who is offering the lowest price and/or the broadest terms. As an underwriter, if you are presented with an applicant who has changed D&O Insurance carriers frequently over the past five or 10 years, a red flag should go up. This is a company you might do well to avoid.

There's an old saying in romantic relationships, "You lose 'em how you got 'em." It's equally true in insurance relationships. If you acquire a new account solely because you've undercut the incumbent carrier's price, the odds are fairly high that someday you'll lose that same account to a competitor's cheaper deal. Buying business by simply undercutting competitors' prices is not an ideal way to run an underwriting business.

Frequency

Some lines of business within the professional lines insurance world are known, with respect to claims, as "high-frequency lines of business."[9] It's expected that these lines of coverage are going to garner a fair number of claims during each policy period. Broker/Dealer E&O Insurance and Insurance Agents E&O Insurance would be two products that fall into this category, especially when they're written for companies with a large workforce. D&O Insurance, however, is decidedly *not* a high-frequency line of business.

Well, it's not supposed to be, anyway.

D&O Insurance claims are generally expected by insurers to be few and far between, especially for well-run companies. However, when D&O claims do arise, insurers

---

[9] Sometimes they're also called "low-severity, high-frequency lines of business," although the "low severity" part is often just wishful thinking on the part of underwriters.

understand that they have the potential to be expensive to resolve, especially if they involve securities class actions against publicly-traded corporations. Privately held companies and not-for-profit organizations generally incur D&O claims that are much less expensive to resolve than those of public companies. More on that in the next subsection.

One point that merits clarification with respect to the claims frequency issue under a D&O Insurance policy: I'm talking here about pure D&O Insurance-type claims, such as those alleging poor management, a precipitous stock price decline and things of that nature. Don't be confused by the fact that many of today's D&O Insurance policies contain a lot of extra "bells and whistles," such as Employment Practices Liability Insurance ("EPLI"), Public Relations or "Crisis" Insurance, Investigative Coverage, etc. Sometimes these policies are written in a "modular structure" so that carriers can "plug in" additional coverages at the insured's request. So, for example, if a large corporation with thousands of employees experiences a sizable number of employment practices-related claims under its D&O Insurance policy, those aren't considered to be traditional D&O claims and should not be counted as such during the underwriting process. Generally, larger companies will have significant self-insured retentions under their D&O Insurance policies, so it often makes more sense, if they want meaningful ancillary coverages, such as EPLI, to purchase separate stand-alone policies to focus on those exposures.

Severity

It's not unusual for D&O Insurance claims to be very expensive, especially for publicly traded corporations facing securities class actions. These types of claims, usually triggered when a company's stock price drops, can have their genesis in any number of issues. Among some of the more common: Poor management decisions, disappointing performance of a key revenue-producing product or service or an inability to keep up with the competition in a company's industry. Mergers and acquisitions which fail – or even those that are simply less-than-totally-successful – also provide rich fodder for plaintiffs' lawyers pursuing the large paydays that can accompany a securities class action.[10]

Some D&O Insurance underwriters operate under the belief that once a company has endured a serious securities class action – or a significant D&O Insurance claim of any nature for that matter – the company becomes a better risk because it has "learned its lesson" and will take the necessary precautions to avoid future problems. One carrier, in particular, was known in the late 1990s and early 2000s for specializing in providing comparably attractive (but still expensive) quotes to insureds right after they suffered limit losses – despite an unwritten (and often unspoken) industry

---

[10] And let's face it, many securities class actions are driven by lawyers seeking fees. If you've ever been part of a class of plaintiffs in a securities class action, you know that filing a claim can be a complex and arduous process and the returns are paltry compared to what you've lost – and what the lawyers get paid.

"rule" that an insurer who pays a limit loss should be given every opportunity to maintain its relationship with the insured in order to earn back its money over time. It's considered a violation of this unwritten rule for competing carriers to undercut an incumbent's price or offer significantly broader terms after the incumbent carrier has paid a limit loss (or just a very large loss, even if it doesn't consume the entire policy limit).

This perception that once an insured company suffers a limit loss under its D&O Insurance it's a safe bet for the foreseeable future is, as you might guess, not really accurate. Off the top of my head, I can think of an insured while I was at AIG who cost us a $25 million limit loss in each of two consecutive policy years for totally unrelated matters. And, certainly, many other insureds have rung the bell for more than one significant D&O Insurance loss in a relatively short period, if not exactly consecutive policy years. As a lot of underwriters learn the hard way, there are no guarantees in the world of D&O Insurance.

Having said that, it is important to look beneath the surface to determine exactly what caused a company's major D&O loss and examine what, if anything, the applicant has done to rectify the situation and ensure that it doesn't recur. There are many cases where a company that has been hit with a big loss (or an "expensive lesson" as some call it) has changed the way it does things in order to avoid repeating history with a similar hit to its bottom line. But, of course, that company can also suffer another big loss for reasons wholly apart from those behind the most recent loss. Again, there are no guarantees.

One of the keys to reviewing the loss history of an applicant that has had a major loss is to assess the overall risk-management strategies put into place by the company after it has suffered the large loss, in order to determine if the company learned a broader lesson and has not merely applied a Band-Aid to one particular problem while turning a blind eye to others.

Another thing to focus on when reviewing the loss history of a D&O Insurance applicant is to do just that – review its loss history, not just its D&O Insurance claims history. There's an important difference between claims history and loss history, especially in the world of D&O Insurance.

Strictly speaking, a D&O Insurance underwriter who is solely interested in reviewing a company's claims history would only look at D&O Insurance claims and not other types of losses. This might make sense for an underwriter of other specialized lines of commercial insurance. For example, a boiler and machinery underwriter really needs to focus on the past performance of the applicant company's boilers and machinery that would be covered by a proposed policy. D&O Insurance underwriters, on the other hand, need to take a much broader view of past losses because virtually any loss, regardless of its origin or nature, could lead to a D&O Insurance claim, especially for publicly-traded companies.

Let's stick with our boiler and machinery example for a minute. Assume that a publicly traded hospitality company purchased a large number of boilers from a manufacturer and, unbeknownst to the hospitality company, they all had a significant latent defect. The hospitality company did no research into the customer reviews or independent laboratory ratings of these boilers. If those boilers all started malfunctioning at the same time, exploding perhaps and causing significant property damage, thereby forcing the hospitality company to close many of its hotels for prolonged and costly repairs, the company's revenues would suffer. Thus, that boiler problem could cause a decline in the company's stock price.

It doesn't require much imagination to envision how a plaintiff's lawyer could argue that poor management decisions in choosing those particular boilers led to a significant disruption in the hospitality company's revenue stream. This scenario might well manifest itself in the form of a D&O Insurance claim.

So, as you can see, it's vital for a D&O Insurance underwriter to review all major losses of an applicant company over a previous period of time, usually three to five years, in order to get a feel for the company's particular challenges and to try to determine if other losses might arise that could lead to D&O Insurance claims.

It's also important for underwriters to confirm that severe losses in the past have been conclusively settled with no likelihood of being resurrected. In this vein, underwriters should also inquire as to whether any follow-on lawsuits might be filed by stakeholders who might not be happy with the matter's conclusion. For example, if a company settles an employment practices class action for more money than some observers think reasonable and the stock price drops, shareholders might later bring a securities class action, alleging that mismanagement of the employment practices claim hurt the company's finances and caused a stock-price decline.

A consistent theme underlying sound underwriting (and also underlying this book) is that good underwriters take a holistic view in order to consider issues from every angle before drawing conclusions. In the preceding example, it would be a serious mistake for an underwriter to simply say "Great, that employment practices case is behind the company now, there's no need to be concerned about it anymore," without digging deeper to discover that disgruntled shareholders have been threatening to sue because they disagreed with the decision to settle the case for that amount of money. By taking that approach, the underwriter would fail to consider an essential element of the applicant company's D&O Insurance risk profile, which, of course, could come back to haunt him.

A side note: Anyone interested in surveying trends in D&O Insurance claims and getting an idea of significant losses with respect to companies across a wide spectrum would be well served to review Advisen's Loss Insight (www.advisen.com). This database contains information on more than 200,000 loss events and over 20 million litigation dockets spanning a variety of insurance products, including

D&O Insurance and other professional lines (as well as virtually every other line of insurance). If you want to use prior loss events to determine how much value can be eroded by another hypothetical loss event, there is no better source.

5. *Structuring a Quote (From Both an Insurer's and Insured's Perspective)*

There are some basic rules (mostly unwritten, until now) for structuring quotes in the world of D&O Insurance. But before we get to those, an underwriter's initial consideration is whether they actually want to offer a quote or, rather, simply an indication. There's a difference.

As even non-insurance people know, a quote is an offer of coverage that may be accepted and bound by the applicant in order to form the basis of an insurance policy. An "indication," on the other hand, in industry parlance, is merely an indication of what the carrier might quote – but it's not bindable. An indication can be thought of as, and is sometimes called, a "ballpark quote;" it reflects the terms and pricing at which the carrier could possibly offer a deal, but there's no guarantee.

Usually, when an insurer offers an indication it's because the insurer believes it lacks some critical information necessary to formulate a concrete, bindable quote. This missing information could be, for example, the applicant company's most recent financial statements or more specific information regarding its loss history. And, of course, a carrier may offer an indication but then later decline to provide a bindable quote once it has reviewed the additional information.

Throughout this book I've talked about taking a "holistic" approach when underwriting; that is, reviewing an applicant from many perspectives and considering a multitude of factors. This works well for larger companies, and even many mid-sized entities, but for smaller accounts a comprehensive underwriting review is often unwarranted and unnecessary. When engaging in "black-box underwriting" of small, relatively straightforward accounts, there's no need to engage in deep analytical thought. These accounts are generally fairly generic, each possessing the same general risk profiles and warranting the same or similar quotes as other applicants falling within their general risk pool. But for our purposes in this section, we'll focus on larger and more complex risks.

Appropriate Limits of Liability

Deciding upon an appropriate limit of liability for D&O Insurance coverage is usually a difficult decision for an insured and its broker. Nobody ever truly knows how much insurance they need ... until they need it. If a company doesn't don't have a D&O claim during the policy year, then its management will feel the company wasted money by purchasing too much insurance. If the company has a severe D&O claim that threatens to exceed its limit of liability, then the risk manager is criticized for not buying high enough limits. A risk manger's (or other insurance purchaser's) job is never easy.

There are various yardsticks that an insured company may use when trying to determine an appropriate limit of liability for its particular risk profile.

A basic method is to simply poll a company's board of directors and senior executives to determine what reasonable D&O Insurance limit of liability would make them comfortable based on their perception of the risks faced by the company and the assets that could be lost by both the company and the individual insureds in a worst-case-scenario claim. Of course, this is not a scientific method, and a risk manager might end up with a lot of requests for very high – and expensive – limits. One would expect that those polled would give answers indicating their level of comfort to attain "sleep insurance" status, that is, enough insurance limits to help them sleep at night.

A second method, grounded in a bit more logic, is one I've seen advocated by some individuals with respect to the purchasing practices of publicly-traded companies. I'll call it the Market Cap Drop Strategy (or "MCD Strategy"). I don't think there's an official name for it, so I will coin one here.

To employ the MCD Strategy, one starts by trying to determine the amount of the largest likely decline in a company's market capitalization (or "cap"). Keep in mind we're not talking about the worst-case scenario, just the most likely. When this figure is established, the next step would be to calculate a certain percentage of that amount, since securities class action suits never settle dollar-for-dollar at the exact amount of the market-cap decline. (At least I've never seen that happen, but I guess it's possible that it has occurred at some point.) A figure I've heard advocated for this part of the equation on more than one occasion is 30 percent. Once 30 percent of the most likely market-cap drop is calculated, the next step would be to use another percentage of that number to arrive at the amount of D&O Insurance limits of liability that the company should buy. I believe 10 percent is a fairly common number here. It's important to keep in mind, however (ah, a disclaimer, a staple of the insurance industry!) that these are only general numbers and that each insured company should make its own determinations, in consultation with its broker, based upon its unique risk factors and other considerations (e.g. preferences of the board of directors, specific industry loss trends, etc.)

I have not run the numbers lately to see how the average securities class-action settlement stacks up under this formula, but it's fairly easy to calculate current norms at any given time if you know the amount of a company's market capitalization decline and the amount of the corresponding settlement of any securities class action lawsuit filed as a result thereof.

No one method is perfect for every company in determining appropriate D&O Insurance limits of liability. Obviously, a wide variety of factors need to be taken into account. However, an excellent tool to assist in this analysis would be comprehensive benchmarking information of peer-group companies, such as those available through most large insurance brokerage firms. These analyses compare companies based upon market cap, industry niches and a variety of other factors. One problem with using brokerage data, however, is that the sampling usually only comes from that brokerage's clients. Using a more universal source, such as Advisen's expansive database of over 3 million insurance programs (www.advisen.com) or the RIMS Benchmark Survey™ of RIMS member firms produced by Advisen (www.RIMS.org/book) can be of great value. These reports are possibly the gold standards of insurance benchmarking – and not just for limits of liability but also for other metrics, such as retentions and premium costs. Regardless of how much data you want to sample, both Advisen and the RIMS Benchmark Survey™ compare peer data among a large number of companies without the limitation of only sampling the clients of one specific brokerage.

Benchmarking is not the be-all/end-all tool for selecting an appropriate limit of liability, of course, although it can provide meaningful guidance as to what one's competitors are doing and may help determine what "best practices" are within an industry niche. A risk manager or other person charged with the insurance purchasing for a company must take into account the unique exposures of that particular company, including, but not limited to (classic insurance language!), the size of the company, nature of the business, largest potential exposure to any one customer or group of customers, market cap (for publicly traded companies; investors' total equity would be a good measuring stick for private companies), geographic footprint (e.g. certain states and foreign countries have judicial and regulatory environments that are particularly hostile or favorable to businesses) and a variety of other things.

A general rule, one that has traditionally, although not always, been observed in the D&O Insurance industry dictates that carriers should never quote a greater limit of liability on the first excess layer of coverage than the primary carrier has quoted (or bound). The exact logic behind this may never be known, but one school of thought is that an excess carrier doesn't want the insured to have an incentive to strike a deal with the primary carrier whereby the primary carrier "rolls over" on a claim in order to allow the insured to access the greater amount of insurance in place on the excess layer. (If you've got a better theory, feel free to write me!) Keep in mind that since the primary carrier drafted the policy and is, presumably, in the best position to interpret it, once it has paid a claim fully it puts more pressure on a follow-form excess carrier to explain why it would justifiably deny coverage for a claim paid in full by the primary carrier.

Naturally, price is one factor that figures into just about every insured company's decision on choosing a limit of liability. Depending upon market conditions, big limits can be very expensive and cause a conflict between obtaining adequate protection for directors and officers while not wasting corporate assets. There are some creative – as "creative" as insurance can be, that is – ways to keep the price down while not sacrificing as much as you might otherwise expect on limits of liability.

Appropriate Retention Levels

One good indicator of an insured company's appetite for risk and its belief it won't have any D&O claims is the size of its self-insured retention (SIR). Some companies, especially larger ones in more volatile industries, are comfortable accepting a very large SIR. Others like the comfort of knowing that their D&O carrier is going to respond with payments very early in the claims process and, thus, they don't mind paying a higher premium for a smaller SIR. To some extent, it's a matter of individual taste, although certainly not exclusively.

Some carriers have minimum SIR levels, especially in very actuarially-driven lines of business. These carriers believe it isn't prudent to write a certain type of risk without a minimal level of protection from claim payments via a specific SIR.

Determining the right SIR, from an insured's perspective, can be very difficult at times. The CEO and majority of the board may have very different ideas than the CFO and/or risk manager. When it's not directly coming out of a budget for which she's responsible, most individual insureds are happy getting the lowest D&O Insurance SIR and highest limit of liability available. Independent directors especially tend to feel this way.

While there is no one "right" answer as to the appropriate SIR level for an insured company, some people have attempted over the years to reduce the decision to a formula. One major financial institution for which I managed the underwriting on while at AIG in the late 1990s pursued an SIR strategy conceived by its CFO. He decided that his company would be comfortable absorbing a loss through the payment of an SIR that was the equivalent of one penny per outstanding share of the company's stock. I don't think he ever revealed (not to me anyway) why the one-penny-per-share SIR was ideal but, as it turned out, the number was within our underwriting guidelines, so we went with it. Sometimes things just work out like that.

Peer benchmarking is also, obviously, a helpful tool in determining an appropriate SIR level for D&O Insurance. While every company is unique, it can be helpful in troubled times to be able to explain to your board of directors that you carry a D&O SIR that is very similar to those of your closest competitors (assuming, of course, that you know those numbers with certainty.)

Some companies try to choose an SIR that won't have a meaningful impact to earnings or cash flow. Market conditions will also influence SIR levels. In a soft (and competitive) D&O Insurance market, carriers may not provide enough of a premium credit/discount to make it worthwhile for an insured company to increase its SIR by a meaningful amount.

From an insurance carrier's perspective, the right SIR to quote is usually determined by a set underwriting formula which can then be tweaked depending upon certain empirical factors as well as the insured's preferences. For example, a carrier may have a formula that states that a company with $1 billion in assets that seeks a $25 million primary layer limit of liability must carrier at least a $1 million SIR. If the insured should desire a higher SIR, a discount can be applied to the premium based on the amount by which the SIR is increased. Each carrier will have their own formula but generally speaking, a doubling of the SIR to $2 million in the example above will not produce a 50 percent discount on the premium for the $25 million limit of liability. If forced to provide a ballpark guess on that number, I would speculate that the discount would be about 5 percent to 7 percent for increasing a $1 billion asset company's SIR from $1 million to $2 million. But, again, a lot of factors would come into play, including specific market conditions, nature of the insured's business, the insured's loss history, etc.

Choosing Your Carrier(s)

One of the most important decisions an insured can make with respect to its insurance program is choosing the right carrier. It might well be *the* most important decision.

I'm a firm believer in the proposition that no carrier is the right choice for every insured; there is no "one size fits all" solution. A variety of factors come into play when an insured is selecting an insurance carrier for its D&O Insurance program, whether it's to lead the program as the primary carrier or merely to write an excess layer. This decision carries special weight for risk managers (or other insurance-buying decision makers) because, as we know, D&O Insurance provides personal protection to a company's senior management and board of directors – and nobody wants to be blamed for choosing a subpar carrier to provide that protection. Here are some factors to consider.

- *Big Insurer vs. Small Insurer* - This category crosses over some of the others above. Basically, a big insurer with a stellar financial rating and the ability to write many different exposures in the U.S. and overseas is more attractive to large companies and smaller companies that hope to be large someday. A smaller insured with only a need for "boutique" underwriting doesn't have to consider the Big Boys for its D&O Insurance program, but it's still a factor to consider for all buyers of insurance.

- *Breadth of Product Offerings* - An insured's overall relationship with a carrier counts for a lot, despite the fact that most insurers say that an insurance relationship is "not a bank account." It's my firm belief that the more lines of coverage you have with a carrier and the more premium you fork over to it, the better your chances of getting a gray-area claim paid. It's well known that almost all carriers that offer both homeowners' insurance and auto coverage provide a discount to insureds who buy both products from the one carrier. This discount is offered because the overall relationship is being enlarged and strengthened. The same concept holds true in professional lines and extends into claims service. If you can place your D&O, E&O, EPL, Fidelity Bonds, etc., with one carrier, the odds are that you'll have a stronger relationship and get more favorable treatment on both premiums and claims handling. Thus, if you place your D&O with an insurer who only writes that line of coverage, or just one or two others, you won't have the opportunity to leverage a larger relationship. This shouldn't be the overriding factor in your choice of carriers, but it should certainly be a consideration. Also, you want a carrier who will be able to provide solutions to your company as you grow, whether domestically, internationally, or both.

- *Claims Reputation* - Claims handling, as people often say in the insurance industry (I do anyway), is where the "rubber meets the road." It's nice to buy a broadly worded and inexpensive insurance policy, but if it provides no coverage when you have a claim, then what's the point? When choosing a carrier for a coverage as important to a company's senior management as D&O Insurance, it's important to make sure that the carrier has a good claims reputation and will handle your claims fairly and promptly. A smart move, although relatively few insureds seem to do it, is to ask for client references from prospective carriers. In particular, you'd like to speak with their insureds who have had claims paid (not just filed but paid) within the past two or three years. When you speak with the people at those companies you should be able to get a feel for how the carrier treats its insureds. If a carrier refuses to provide references, it may be a warning sign that you're dealing with an insurer who plays hardball once a claim is filed. Your broker should also be able to offer an opinion on various carriers' claims handling practices, although sometimes brokers try to skirt the issue. This is because they'd like to avoid making enemies of carriers of whom they have a negative opinion. (Note: Secrets are rare in the insurance industry, and you should always assume that everything you say *will* get around.) Brokers also may not want to be blamed for recommending a carrier whose claims department later proves to be difficult. Nonetheless, if you force the issue, you should be able to get some insights from your broker – otherwise, get a new broker.

- *Financial Strength* - While just about every carrier will tout its financial strength in one way or another (and most brokerage firms won't recommend to a client a carrier with weak financials), there have been insurance carriers who've gone from having a good financial rating from one or more of the rating agencies to insolvency in fairly short order. It can happen. Most clients seem to draw the line at carriers having an A.M. Best rating of at least A-minus, although more discerning buyers, especially pension funds, some financial institutions and some government-related entities, may require a minimal rating of "A." I'd recommend that insurance buyers review multiple ratings assigned to a carrier by various ratings agencies; relying on just one rating opinion can be misleading. Insurance buyers should also conduct their own independent review of a carrier's financial strength if the insurance being purchased is important enough. In the past, I've been involved with insureds who request conference calls or meetings with my employer's CFO or other finance executives in order to review financial strength issues.

Also, sometimes financially-troubled insurers will put in place a "cut through" in order to stay in business. This is a guarantee from another carrier that it will step up to pay the troubled carrier's claims should it become insolvent. I've had limited experience with this phenomenon, but my advice would be to avoid carriers who need to resort to this tactic. There are usually enough financially-solvent carriers in the insurance marketplace that an insured needn't worry about dealing with an impaired carrier that has to rely on a third-party guarantor. Plus, who knows how the claims would be handled, and by whom, if the third party actually had to step up to provide funding?

- *Length of Time in the Market* - Carriers seem to enter and depart from the D&O Insurance market constantly. . I can think of a number of carriers who, after achieving success in other lines of insurance, such as auto or homeowners', take a mountain of cash and jump into the D&O market. These carriers are usually attracted to D&O Insurance by the product's long tail for claims payments. These carriers can collect a lot more investment income on premium payments under a D&O policy while a claim drags on for six years than they could collect on the premium from an auto insurance policy whose claim is settled within three months of being made. So before committing to a carrier, I'd advise insureds to investigate how committed that carrier is to the D&O market. Having to shop around for a new D&O policy a year or two after initially binding with a carrier who exited the market negates any goodwill and "money in the bank" that the insured had built up with that exiting carrier. It may also cause the insured's board of directors and senior management to question the competence of the risk manager (or other individual insurance buyer) who recommended using a carrier that was not long for the market.

- *Name Recognition* - This factor applies to the selection of both an insurance carrier and an insurance broker – sometimes. Name recognition of carriers and brokers usually carries more weight when the insured is a larger company with a distinguished board of wealthy and/or high-profile directors. In these cases, the price of D&O Insurance is often not as important as placating the board with D&O Insurance written by a company they're familiar with and trust. A very wealthy board member may be perfectly comfortable with an AIG, Zurich or ACE writing their coverage, but if the risk manager tells that same board member, "Don't worry, you're protected, our D&O Insurance is written by Insolvency Mutual," there's going to be a problem. The same principle applies to the selection of an insurance broker to place the D&O Insurance; boards want to deal with names they're familiar with and who they believe will do a good job based on reputation alone. When a large claim comes in, the risk manager doesn't want to tell his board, "There's no need for concern, our broker, Dewey, Cheatem & Howe, has it under control." Smaller companies, however, frequently don't care about name recognition because they're primarily concerned with getting decent coverage at the lowest price, no matter who can provide it.

- *Personal Relationships* - There are differing schools of thought on this point, but I'm a firm believer that commercial insurance is a relationship business. When you're handing over a six- or seven-figure premium to someone, it's human nature to want to know them personally and trust them. When you're an insured facing a $5 million claim, you don't want to call a nameless customer-service rep and be put on hold. I could cite a fair number of situations where I've seen a personal relationship help get a policy bound or a claim paid. Happens all the time. Having said all that, I also think that one needs to be careful to not put too much weight on personal relationships. For example, people leave companies, and the good buddy of yours who was running the claims department when you bound your policy with a carrier may now work elsewhere, and the new claims manager might not know you from a hole in the wall. Plus, good personal relations only go so far when corporate guidelines kick in and must be followed. Bottom line: I'd advocate placing your business with an insurer who employs at least one or two people who you know and trust, if possible, but don't make it a deal breaker if you don't know anybody working for the carrier who offers you the best overall deal. You can also forge relationships over time.

- *Using The Same Carrier to Lead Two Or More Insurance Programs* - When an insured is purchasing coverage in addition to D&O Insurance, it is often a good idea to use the same carrier to lead the other program as well, especially if the other coverage is another professional line of insurance, such as E&O Insurance. Sometimes a single claim can implicate coverage under both a D&O Insurance and an E&O Insurance policy and the insured does not want to be put in a position of standing by while the lead carriers on each program point fingers at each other, alleging that the claim is only covered under the other carrier's policy and therefore it's only the other carrier's responsibility to pay. By having the same carrier lead both lines of insurance, this possibility is eliminated. D&O Insurance claims can also cross lines with other types of policies, including Pension Trust (or ERISA) Insurance, Employment Practices Liability Insurance and Fidelity Bonds, depending upon the specific wording of the policies and the facts of the claim.

- *Willingness to Manuscript* - Some carriers tend to be more rigid and unyielding than others when it comes to customizing, or "manuscripting" as we say in the industry, coverage for the particular needs of an insured. This is especially true in a hard market where carriers may assume a take-it-or-leave-it approach. Fortunately for insureds and brokers, there haven't been many hard markets in the past 25 years or so. Nonetheless, some carriers are more conservative than others. For example, a conservative carrier might refuse to extend coverage for new exposures outside of a traditional D&O Insurance policy's parameters no matter how much additional premium is offered. Thus, dynamic companies expecting to grow significantly would be wise to select a carrier who can grow with them. Such insured companies need carriers who can offer both a diversity of insurance products and sizeable limits of liability.

Ideas to Reduce Premiums for Insureds and Claims Expenses for Carriers

Coinsurance - Coinsurance is an arrangement that requires an insured to retain responsibility for a portion of every paid loss all the way up to a policy's full limit of liability. Thus, for example, assume that an insured purchases a D&O Insurance policy with a $10 million limit of liability, a 10 percent coinsurance feature and a $100,000 SIR. Let's further assume that the insured sustains a fully covered (i.e. no allocation) loss of $200,000. After the application of the $100,000 SIR, there would be $100,000 of covered loss remaining. The insured would then be required to pay 10 percent of every dollar above the SIR. Since there is $100,000 of insured loss above the SIR, the carrier would write a check for $90,000 and the insured would be on the hook for the remaining $10,000 as its coinsurance payment. NOTE: This is the way most coinsurance works through U.S.-based carriers. London markets generally apply coinsurance in a different manner, but I'm going to skip that to avoid confusion (or at least avoid more than I've already caused!). Suffice it to say, however, that "London-style" coinsurance works to reduce the actual limit of liability available to pay the claim while U.S.-style coinsurance merely stretches out that limit of liability so that it will take a larger loss to completely exhaust it. London-style coinsurance is explained more fully in this book's Glossary.

Defense-Only Coverage - Many times insureds, brokers and carriers don't think about this, but purchasing coverage that responds only to pay defense costs of a claim can save an insured significant money in the right circumstances. Legal fees continue to rise and, as many people familiar with D&O claims know, it's not unusual for the total cost of defense, including those arising from discovery practice, expert-witness fees, and other related costs (such as copying, paying for deposition transcripts, etc.) to exceed the value of a settlement or judgment. By buying a policy that only pays for defense costs, an insured can still address a major concern but save a substantial portion of its premium costs. Of course, this could prove to be a bad idea if a claim leads to a large verdict or settlement, but with defense costs covered an insured may be more likely to fight a claim until the end (or at least until the insurance coverage maxes out) and, possibly, prevail. Defense-only policies are certainly not for everyone, but they do provide great value for some insureds in particular situations.

"Corridor Retentions" or "Vented Layers" - An option that brokers and insureds seldom consider is the concept of using a Corridor Retention or creating Vented Layers. Where there is an interim SIR between layers of coverage, those layers of coverage are said to be "Vented Layers." This structure involves inserting one or more self-insured layers between layers of insurance coverage in a multi-layered tower. So, for example, assume an insured company wants to purchase limits of liability stretching all the way up to cover a potential $100 million loss, but the aggregate premium costs turn out to be prohibitive. The insured may elect to self-insure a couple of those layers, such as the $10 million layer in excess of $50 million and the $10 million layer in excess of $80 million. While the insured will not get as much "credit" against the premium prices as it would by retaining an extra $20 million of an SIR at the bottom of the tower, it will pay less than it would have had it purchased an entire $100 million tower of coverage. The insured company can still tell board members (and analysts and other interested parties) that it has D&O coverage that reaches the $100 million mark; it's just that the coverage isn't continuous all the way up the tower.

Companies sometimes elect to purchase programs featuring Corridor Retentions or Vented Layers because they want to spread available limits over a greater vertical distance to secure coverage at a higher layer than the company might otherwise be able to afford. It may also need to do so in response to certain carriers – especially those who are traditionally reinsurers and/or are more conservative – who are willing to provide capacity for a large program but refuse to attach below a certain point. If there's not enough other capacity available to reach that minimum attachment point, the insured may have no other viable choice but to use a

Corridor Retention in order to attract the conservative carrier's capacity.

Unwritten (Until Now) Rules for Quoting D&O Insurance

There are certain unstated rules that good D&O Insurance underwriters follow in quoting accounts. Some are just common sense and others are not, but they are all worth considering. One of the themes running through this book, as you no doubt have gathered by now, is that D&O Insurance is an art as well as a science; therefore, there is some room to bend, or totally break, rules on a case-by-case basis depending upon particular circumstances. Nonetheless, as the Dalai Lama once supposedly said (disclaimer: I couldn't verify this): "Know the rules well, so you can break them effectively." Here are a few of the more valuable unwritten rules.

- *When Quoting Primary, Try To Get A "Look-Up" Endorsement* - This will enable you to see what ILF (see Glossary) the carriers above you are getting. You don't want to be embarrassed (and cheated) by being paid a lower rate-per-million than other insurers attaching above you. Also, a carrier above you may have an important exclusion or other term or condition that you lack. There are not too many things more embarrassing to an underwriter (and damaging to his career) than having to pay a claim on the primary layer for something that is excluded by all of the excess carriers.

- *Issue Every Quote With An Expiration Date* - Quotes, like bread, fruit and vegetables, can get stale. And situations

change. Smart underwriters force applicants to make a
decision by imposing an expiration date on each quote.
Also, you should always make the quote rescindable in case
you discover an adverse fact before the quote has been
bound (or even thereafter; check with your legal counsel on
this; again, I am NOT providing legal advice in this book...)

- *Include Copies of All Endorsements With The Quote* - I've
  seen far too many disputes arise from the fact that a carrier
  quoted an endorsement using shorthand (e.g. "specific
  claim exclusion") without providing the EXACT wording
  until after the account was bound. Eliminate all
  opportunities for those kinds of misunderstandings by
  providing the exact wording up front, BEFORE the
  applicant gives the order to bind.

- *Never Quote A Higher Limit On An Excess Layer Than
  The Amount of the Primary Layer* - This rule was told to
  me very early in my underwriting career (possibly by Fred
  Flintstone, I don't remember.) The logic behind this is that
  you never want a carrier below you to pay its lower limit in
  a situation where it is unwarranted because the insured
  struck a deal with the lower-positioned carrier in order to
  get at your larger layer of excess coverage. When you're
  writing excess coverage, you want the primary carrier to
  have at least as much skin in the game as you when a claim
  is filed. It makes sense if you think about it, trust me.

- *When Quoting Excess, Be Clear As To Whether You Are
  Following Form Or Providing Difference-In-Conditions
  (DIC) Coverage* - This is another area that gives rise to a

surprisingly-large number of disputes. The commercial insurance world is rife with the exchange of insurance shorthand and "I-have-to-make-this-quick-because-I'm-busy" pronouncements which don't always address every critical issue. When quoting excess coverage, it's imperative that carriers spell out exactly what their terms will be.

One Piece of Good Advice

I thought it would be valuable to readers of this book, almost all of whom are likely to be fairly new to insurance, or new to the professional lines segment of insurance anyway, to receive career advice from some of the brightest and most-respected minds in the industry. To that end, I asked a number of successful insurance executives to provide one piece of career advice to industry newcomers. Preferably something that they wish they'd known when they were starting their careers.

None of the people quoted below read this book before providing their wisdom, therefore, I must emphatically state that none of them endorse, or necessarily agree with, anything I've written herein. Also, all opinions expressed below are those of the person who provided them and should not be attributed to their employers or anyone else. Each person quoted below shares a desire to give back to this industry that has been so good to many of us.

In addition, the executives quoted below participated in this exercise (which, unfortunately for them, entailed receiving several long-winded emails from me) in order to support the six charities benefiting from revenue generated by this book. I greatly appreciate their generosity of spirit, as do, I'm sure, the six charities. It is not an act of false modesty when I say that this chapter will benefit readers more than any other in this book, and for that I sincerely thank each of the individuals quoted below.

Steven Anderson – Senior Insurance Executive:

"When asked why he didn't pick those who were generally regarded to be the best collegiate hockey players for the 1980 U.S. Olympic team, Herb Brooks supposedly responded, "I'm not looking for the best players. I'm looking for the best team." (Moral: How you interact with others and how you fit into the overall picture is often more important than natural ability; so be a great teammate.)"

Richard J. Barquist – Vice President, Global Corporate Risk Management, MetLife, Inc.:

"In my experience, the first question from a member of a board of directors about D&O coverage is never about the cost."

David Bell – President & CEO, ALPS Corporation:

"Find someone in the industry who really understands technical language and who has witnessed the carnage of loss examples. Stay close to that person and learn from their experience and history. Otherwise, history will surely repeat itself – for you."

George Biancardi – President & CEO, Strongwood Insurance Holdings Corp:

"Always give 100 percent and don't take short cuts. Assume that you will be remunerated for your constant hard work after the fact, not in advance. If you've been giving it your all and your employer does not adequately reward you, then you should find another employer who will. But never stop giving it your all or that will diminish your value."

Phil Blais – Chairman and Founder, Blais Excess and Surplus:

"Success in insurance is only achieved by those who consider themselves a student of insurance, regardless of tenure. And never hide, lie or alter your actions while serving as an insurance professional."

Stephen J. Burnhope – Deputy Chairman, Financial and Professional, Arthur J. Gallagher (UK) Limited:

"Initially, I would offer three pieces of advice to industry newcomers. First, never pretend that you understand something that you don't. Second, remember that we are paid for what we do, not for who we are. And third, realize that brand names and brochures don't do insurance business, people do."

Richard Cagney – CEO, Cagney Research Group:

"Leave your ego at the door when you come in. Never view yourself as 'selling' a product. Always view what you do as helping improve one's lot in life and truly focus on that person's needs. Two of the biggest impediments to long term success are egos and arrogance. Get rid of them. Always do what is right and just. Follow up and do what you say you are going to do and when you said you were going to do it. Apologize when it's necessary. Treat people with dignity, respect, and love. That is the way you would like to be treated. Network, network, network – all the time. Always have cards with you."

Scott Carmilani – Chairman, Chief Executive Officer and President, Allied World Assurance Company Holdings, A.G.:

"One must be careful during any transaction as there is usually a surprise, and usually it's an unpleasant one."

Carmelo Casella – Managing Director, Corporate Insurance Group, The Bank of New York Mellon:

"Never make a promise regarding any aspect of the business that you cannot keep; it's important to always manage people's expectations."

Christopher J. Cavallaro – Co-Founder, ARC Excess & Surplus, LLC:

"Work hard and be nice...Always help those in need and take time to help the young people in this business as your generosity will come back to you tenfold."

Jeffrey M. Cohen – EVP & Chief Marketing Solutions Officer, Advisen Ltd.:

"I am delighted to offer my best advice to new entrants in the P&C insurance arena. Whether you are marketing a new product, policy language, a broker service, or some other insurance aspect, my first rule of thumb is to differentiate the product. That means that you need to define its unique attributes and emphasize them. Also, when it comes to positioning yourself with colleagues, clients, and even competitors, be sure to take this same approach. You are more likely to be remembered on the sticky part of someone's brain when you demonstrate your qualities which cannot be duplicated. So, be memorable. Second, in my role at Advisen, I send lots of messages to the commercial insurance community via a variety of mediums such as email. From a marketing perspective, that's important, but it's more important that you are responsive, so take the time to reply thoughtfully to every inquiry. It gets noticed. Larry asked me to convey my best piece of advice, so I am responding. And lastly, deliver more than what was asked. In commercial settings, this is called value-add. In underwriting, brokerage, and risk management settings, anticipate the next question or request, and provide that, too. Give back more than was requested. Larry asked me for one thing; if you're reading this though, then he printed these three items with which I responded. I'm giving you my three best pieces of advice. Good Luck!"

Robert C. Cox – Executive Vice President, Chubb & Son, Inc.:

"This is a great business combining financial, statistical, legal, marketing and communication skills along with a healthy dose of gut instinct to be successful. A good understanding of human behavior sure helps as well! I've always found that this business offers the opportunity to be creative and entrepreneurial for those who want to be. Given the inevitable ups and downs, a thick skin and sense of humor are indispensable!"

Lance Dalzell-Piper – Senior Insurance Executive:

"I'd advise underwriters to never write a D&O policy for a public company or financial institution for longer than 12 months (plus odd time if need be). No money can be charged to cover the potential changes that take place in a short time within organizations."

Lisa Doherty – President and CEO, Business Risk Partners:

"I have always been amazed at the scope of skills required to be a good broker or underwriter. In addition to the art of deal making, professionals in our industry need financial analytical skills, legal knowledge, relationship building talents and probably most importantly, the common sense to bring that all together. There are very few jobs, particularly early in one's career, that afford that kind of diversity of content. It is one reason I am still passionate about what I do 25 years later,

I am always learning. My advice to new entrants into our field is to appreciate that variety - rather than let it overwhelm. If you can master the component parts, it will lead to a long, varied, engaging and successful career."

James Drinkwater – President, AmWINS Brokerage:

"If you can rely on one constant in this industry, it is change. It seems like we devote a great deal of time and energy trying to predict market cycles – when they will change, by how much, and for how long – sadly our predictions are rarely correct and there is little that we, as a broker, can do to change the market but prepare ourselves and our clients. As a wholesaler, our clients are always looking for a competitive edge and for us to be successful we need to become a valued partner that is as deeply invested in their success as we are in our own. I believe that one way to further develop this relationship and become the indispensable partner every client can't do without is by driving toward specialization. With unparalleled expertise in a specific area, you will build a reputation for being able to solve a client's unique needs, delivering a service that no one else can (or is willing to try). It is this skill set that makes you, just as much as anything else, the valuable resource your client depends on, and this will differentiate you in any market, regardless of the cycle."

Brian Duperreault – CEO and President (Retired), Marsh & McLennan Companies, Inc.:

"When you are choosing a company to start your career you have to use your head and your heart. You have to analyze the company's balance sheet and earnings power. More importantly you must judge the intangibles. What is the culture in the company? What are their ethics? Will you thrive in the environment? Trust your instincts."

Merritt Fabel – Risk Manager, Starr Insurance Holdings, Inc.:

"Know your audience. Answer the question "What's in it for them?" Describe sections A, B, C, limits and deductibles and priority of payments (if applicable.) And keep it short."

Jennifer J. Fahey – Chief Broking Officer - U.S. and Americas, Aon Risk Solutions:

"Give of yourself: take every opportunity to guide people with gently delivered, constructive criticism and advice. You have or will benefit from the advice of so many, ensure you similarly help others. Give yourself a broad view and a diversity of ideas: don't surround yourself with people just like you, seek out people of differing gender, age groups, backgrounds and experience and who have complementary skills. Similarly don't set policy for people who you aren't close to – ensure you see the world from their perspective. Avoid isolating yourself in an "ivory tower" – get out there and mix with those you are responsible for, as well as your clients and colleagues. Take risks – seek opportunities to work in other geographies and other businesses. Build a specialization and then go broad. Stay close to revenue drivers for your firm. Take time to ponder needed innovation. Have fun!"

Greg Flood – Chief Executive Officer, IronPro:

"Insurance is a tremendous industry to commit a career to. It's omnipresent and limitless in challenges. Within the constant changes of the economy existing risk increases, it evolves, new risks emerge. That's our opportunity. We are routinely responsive to those changes, trading those risks via a modified existing product or a new product. This industry will consume your curiosity and interest for a lifetime."

Jack Flug – Managing Director, Marsh FINPRO:

"Be honest, authentic and always respectful. And know your limitations, including what you don't know. Never be afraid to ask a question (someone else is ALWAYS thinking the same one.)"

Adrian Fox – Executive Director, Financial Institutions Practice, Arthur J. Gallagher (London):

"My principals have always been to control your time and treat customers/staff/friends in the way in which you too would wish to be treated. Respect everyone – from the cleaner to the tea lady. Politeness is free. And one more thing: probably the best thing I ever did at a young age was to read and re-read Mark McCormack's book – 'What They Didn't Teach You At Harvard Business School;' it's still as good a management book today as it was when he wrote it. There, my secret is out!"

Maurice R. "Hank" Greenberg – Chairman and CEO, Starr Companies*, Former Chairman and CEO, American International Group, Inc.:

"Your request to write a bit of advice to newcomers in the insurance industry is a challenge, not because there is nothing to say, but because there is so much to say.

There are many people who come to the insurance industry with a decent education, some with no education and some with very expensive educations. It really makes no difference what their education level is, rather it is about who they are. You can have the best education and be a flop. You can have a poor education but have the drive and intellect to overcome what you have lacked in a formal education. You need to be inquisitive because what was true in one era will not necessarily be true in future eras.

There are those that shy away from change, and there are others who embrace change. I happen to be one of the later, recognizing that this is where the opportunities are. That is how growth takes place.

Change is constant and if you understand that, you will see new opportunities. Whether in the economy, new industries, new political issues, new uncertainties, revolutions, or even terror threats. All can lead to new opportunities if you are alert to change and can recognize these changes and provide the appropriate or necessary coverage.

You also have to recognize risk and plan accordingly. Whatever exists today will be different a decade from now.

Finally, you must recognize the regulatory environment as well. It can create opportunities or problems, depending upon how it is managed."

*Starr Companies is the worldwide marketing name for the operating insurance and travel assistance companies and subsidiaries of Starr International Company, Inc. and for the investment management business of C.V. Starr & Co., Inc.

Jason Hawkins – Managing Director, Marsh:

"Someone once told me - Your reputation is the only thing you have in this industry – it takes only a second to ruin and a lifetime to repair!"

Dinos Iordanou – CEO and Chairman, Arch Capital Group, Ltd.:

"The advice I give to all of our trainees is to not let a day go by without learning something new. The insurance business is subject to a great deal of specialization that must be learned on the job. Continuous learning is the only path of advancement in our business."

Ralph E. Jones III – CEO, Sparta Insurance Holdings:

"My only words of advice to young professionals would be that...Credibility is the coin of the realm. If you can say what you mean and mean what you say, you will be a lot better off in the long run. It often takes much political courage to do this, but organizations that do well have people like this in abundance. Simply 'doing what you say you are going to do' leads to outstanding performance. It is easy to say but hard to do in a world where many business and political leaders lack these simple values."

Todd J. Jones – Chief Executive Officer, Willis North America:

"In our business, like most businesses, relationships are built on trust, honesty and integrity. You will spend a career building those relationships and your own personal brand that support them, don't lose sight that the foundation never changes – trust, honesty and integrity – and if there's a crack in that foundation, the personal brand you spent years building, will be gone in an instant."

John Kerns – Executive Managing Director, Beecher Carlson:

"My advice would be: 1.) Never let a client feel like you have any other clients; 2.) Take two week vacations whenever you can, they're easier to do early in your career; 3.) Always have a sense of urgency; and 4.) If you're not somewhat stressed and worried that you may not make your timeline, you probably don't have enough to do."

Kevin H. Kelley – Chief Executive Officer, Ironshore, Inc.:

"My advice is: Trust and listen to your gut. Instinct is important, so trust it. Always verify it with a reality check, but whenever in doubt, go with it."

K.C. Kidder – Senior Vice President & Risk Manager (Retired), Wells Fargo & Company:

"Be passionate about what you do and about how much you respect your employer—who you do it for. You obviously must already have the talent, skills and knowledge to have secured your job. Where your passion intersects with your talent, you'll be successful and enjoy what you do—adding immeasurable value to your own life, to your team, and to the results of your employer."

Jack Kuhn – Chief Executive Officer, Endurance Insurance, Endurance Specialty Insurance Ltd.:

"My small piece of advice would be not to be afraid to ask questions to gain a better understanding of an issue. To many times I have seen individuals at all levels afraid to ask questions because they are concerned how it might make them look. One of the keys to success in this business is being well educated. It all starts with asking the right questions."

Dean Klisura – Managing Director/U.S. Risk Practices and Specialties Leader, Marsh:

"Be a voracious reader of key industry news and events. Put yourself in a position to join any topical discussion that is relevant to the industry. In addition, if you are current on news and events you always have a good reason to approach your boss and engage them in a meaningful discussion."

Kevin M. LaCroix, Esq. – Executive Vice President, R-T ProExec, A Division of R-T Specialty, LLC • Author, The D&O Diary Blog:

"Success cannot be guaranteed, but it can be deserved"

Jeff Lattmann – Executive Managing Director, Beecher Carlson:

"I have a few pieces of advice to share: Remember the person you are about to scream at may very well be your next boss. Trust your instincts. Do not allow others to create your reputation, create your own. You live it so own it. One does not have to remember what one said if you always speak the truth. And find a way to make a difference in people's lives and you will be rewarded above and beyond your efforts."

LouAnn Layton – Managing Director, Marsh & McLennan Companies:

"Over the years some very wise and successful folks gave me advice that I have endeavored to utilize in my career. I share them as good reminders to those who are navigating their own careers: Remember every conversation with a senior executive is an interview. When you are given a seat at "the table" take the opportunity to voice your opinions and back them up. Do not be afraid to take on more or greater responsibility before you think you are ready."

John Lumelleau – President and CEO, Lockton, Inc.:

"Choosing a career in insurance is an excellent idea. By joining the insurance industry, you will play a role in promoting, protecting, and securing global commerce. Come in with your eyes wide open, so you can explore the many opportunities in this business. As you build your career, select a specialty and develop your expertise, so you position yourself as an expert. Recognized experts have the greatest visibility within the industry as a whole and are routinely sought out for advancement and new opportunities. Be prepared to make friends, be prepared to have fun, and be prepared to be amazed by the wide range of experiences available in the insurance industry."

James J. Maguire, Jr. – Chairman and CEO (Retired), Philadelphia Insurance Companies:

"I tell young underwriters that insurance is the only business where your cost of goods sold aren't known until some future date. As a result, anyone can sell it, but only those with underwriting discipline survive. And remember, whatever can go wrong, will; so, partner with the best reinsurers."

James J. Maguire, Sr. – Founder and Chairman Emeritus, Philadelphia Insurance Companies:

"Show up every day. Set goals and have dreams...success is a marathon. To be successful, surround yourself with winners. If you hang out with dogs, you'll wake up with fleas."

David McElroy – Chairman and CEO, Arch Worldwide Insurance Group:

"Read as much as you can about as many topics you can from as many sources you can. Common sense and logic are essential skills in our industry, and you will not develop them by just reading insurance manuals, insurance policies and insurance periodicals all the time."

Vince McGeehan – Markel Global Reinsurance:

"No amount of preparation is too much. Anything worthwhile requires preparation."

Stefano Minale – Chief Claims Officer, HCC Insurance Holdings:

"I tell newcomers to the industry to learn as much as they can about all aspects of the business. First, work in claims to get a good understanding of how these policies work. Then try the underwriting side so you understand the business aspects and, finally, try the brokerage side so you can see what the client's needs are. Also, meet and get to know as many people in the industry as you can. There are great opportunities in professional lines of insurance, but the people that are successful are those who try to understand all aspect of the business."

Mike Mitrovic – President, Global Claims, Ironshore:

"The advice I would give to someone entering the insurance world is that it is a great industry. Without it the wheels of commerce would grind to a halt. Networking and relationships are important and your credibility and integrity are your greatest assets. Try to be a problem solver and carry yourself with humility and be respectful of others. It is a marathon and not a sprint and success is built over time."

Phil Norton – Vice Chairman, Midwest Region, Arthur J. Gallagher Risk Management Services, Inc.:

"See and be seen. Opportunities surround you if you know where to look. Be prepared to capitalize by focusing on your strengths and developing them into real expertise. Then, be at the right place at the right time. This can be planned through imperfect estimation – not every meeting turns into something good, at least not right away. Mix patience and persistence with a realistic assessment of potential. And when you are at the right event, make sure the key people notice you and you are also aware of who else made it to the event. This goal may only take you a short amount of time, and that's fine. Enjoy the journey; it is continuous."

Michael O'Connell – Managing Director, Aon Financial Institutions Practice:

"Always aim to understand what's important to your client, anticipate opportunities and challenges for your client today and tomorrow and never forget to listen."

Steve Pincus – Executive Vice President, Willis:

"It is a people business. If you are a people person, you can do very well."

Stan Quirk – Managing Partner, ARC MidAtlantic Excess & Surplus, Inc.:

"My words of advice would be: 1.) Fear no opponent. Respect every opponent; 2.) Remember, it's the perfection of the smallest details that make big things happen; 3.) Keep in mind that hustle makes up for many a mistake; 4.) Be more interested in character than reputation; 5.) Be quick, but don't hurry; 6) Understand that the harder you work, the more luck you will have; 7.) Know that valid self-analysis is crucial for improvement; 8.) Remember that there is no substitute for hard work and careful planning. Failing to prepare is preparing to fail; and 9.) Success is peace of mind that is a direct result of self- satisfaction in knowing you did your best to become the best you are capable of becoming."

John Rafferty – Executive Vice President, Financial & Professional Liability Group, Arch Insurance Group:

"Strategy" is oftentimes over-rated while "Execution" is typically under-appreciated. Most underwriters sound impressive when discussing what they aim to do, but the best have the ability and fortitude to deliver true, quantifiable results differentiation day-in, day-out, year-in, year-out over an extended period of time."

Susan Rivera – President and CEO, V3 Insurance Partners:

"Don't just list the hurdles -- clear the hurdles!"

Evan Rosenberg – Global Specialty Product Manager, Chubb Group of Insurance Companies:

"One of the things that we benefited from was having guys like Al Salvatico, Bill Brown and Jim Wallace willing to mentor our generation. The advice I would give to young underwriters is to spend time with senior folks in and out of their organization to learn the business. Today there is far too little training, everything is a spreadsheet comparison, the art of the deal and the relationship aspect are not valued. Young underwriters should do broker and client visits with senior folks to learn the soft skills - like Floodie always 'forgetting' his pen! They need not know only the right questions to ask, but how to ask them."

Thomas P. Ruggieri – CEO and Co-Founder, Advisen Ltd.:

"Looking back over my 30-year career as an insurance broker and then as the CEO of a firm that provides information and analytics to the insurance community, the characteristic I favor most is something I call 'Creative Tenacity.' For me, this is the ability to see the solution and take the bull by the horns and execute it. I look for evidence of it in every one of our new hires at Advisen. While everything worth doing requires hard work, information and analytics adds another layer of complexity on top.

I miss my deal-making days as an insurance broker. You are never the only person pitching an insurance solution to a client. There's always someone else out there who wants that account, too. Remember, when the business moves, someone gains an account and someone else loses the account. So, your head has got to be in the game. And so does your heart. Play the game like you want to win, and you will win more often than not.

And that leads me to my second point. You need stamina. The commercial insurance business is rapidly becoming global. There's no longer any such thing as just "a day at the office." You need to be ready to serve your client's needs, chase new business, and then go out for a drink with your clients and colleagues, too. That takes stamina. And lastly, you need to use that stamina on the details because the commercial insurance marketplace conducts transactions in the form of agreements, binders, and contracts. In order to best arrange for the outcome you want, you must know the details."

Ty Sagalow – President, Innovation Insurance Group:

"Every major change in the world started with a single creative thought. Think out of the box."

Al Salvatico – Co-Founder of ARC, Retired (But, as Al says, "Still Busy and Loving It!"):

"Always tell clients what they need to know, not what you think they want to hear. It may cost you an insecure client over the years, but it will win and keep you many more clients over the long haul."

Adriaan E. M. Schieferdecker – Managing Director, Bank of America:

"Not many people realize that Property/Casualty Insurance is not an actuarial ideal because accounting rules won't permit that and, so, it really is a relationship business, one of the last areas of business where a handshake means something."

Paul W. Sult III – Hanover Excess and Surplus:

"Find an insurance market niche...whatever it may be, study it, master it, develop expertise in it and become a specialist in it thereby adding value to the insurance buying transaction."

Brian Specht – Chief Underwriting Officer, Aon Affinity:

"When I started in 1988 as a trainee with Chubb, no one wanted to hear about my profession as a D&O/Financial Institutions underwriter. Twenty-five years later, you see D&O issues on the front page of the news, discussed on the sidelines of youth soccer games and talked about at neighborhood dinners."

Giles Stockton – Head of D&O Worldwide, Brit Syndicate at Lloyd's:

"The one quote that I think always gives good advice to someone entering this business on the underwriting side is this: Don't let the scent of the premium mask the stench of the risk."

Vince Tizzio – President and CEO, Navigators Management Company, Inc.:

"You have landed in an industry where you will forever learn, meet interesting people, and provide a great lifestyle for your family or loved ones. Seize the opportunity and always remember people are our greatest asset in the business."

Stephen L. Way – Principal, SLW International, LLC Chairman and CEO, Houston International Insurance Group Founder and Former CEO, HCC Insurance Holdings:

"Our business is cyclical with more average or bad years than good years in each cycle. To build a successful business you must have a platform that performs well in the average or bad years, the good years will take care of themselves. Benjamin Disraeli said 'the thing we learn from history, is that we learn nothing from history'. The insurance industry personifies this."

Alexander Wayne – Founder, Alexander J. Wayne & Associates, Inc.:

"One of the precepts I pass along to my employees: as a wholesale broker: We have many brokers but relatively few markets. Keep that perspective in mind when dealing with those markets. Also, never be the front runner when introducing new insurance products. These are the folks with all the arrows in their backs."

David B. Williams – Vice President, Chubb Specialty Insurance:

"In setting your career goals keep these five issues in mind: 1.) The job or role that you are currently aspiring to may not be the same by the time you are qualified to take the position, so stay in tune with corporate restructuring and market place evolution and reset your aspirations accordingly;

2.) Make a note, actually write it down at least twice a year, of the work activities that make you happy, for example, know if you enjoy customer engagement, managing profit and loss, people or project management, operations or sales and marketing or something different like international work; 3.) Do not be afraid to hitch yourself to a few wagons; once you have determined what makes you happy, identify a leader in those practice areas and let them know you are a disciple and want their guidance and support by conversations, not emails alone; 4.) Corporations are much more likely to provide feedback on your areas for development and improvement; rather than seek validation make sure you cultivate personal professional satisfaction; and 5.) Get to know people outside of work, engagement in professional associations like PLUS help this process. There are great people in the industry, take the time to make friends as you navigate you career journey."

Tom Zacharopoulos – Managing Director, Integro Insurance Brokers:

"My belief is that face to face is always better than using the phone, but the phone is always better than email."

D&O Insurance Glossary

This section contains definitions for some commonly used terms in the D&O Insurance world. Many definitions are also applicable on a wider basis within the insurance industry in general. Some terms below are used in a colloquial manner and many have no precise "official" definition; their meanings will, instead, depend upon specific facts and policy wordings.

Admitted Carrier

An insurer that is licensed and authorized to do business in a particular state on an "admitted basis." In order to obtain this status, a carrier must have its rates and policy forms reviewed and approved by the state's insurance regulatory body. In addition, the carrier must contribute a certain percentage of each premium written in that state toward the state's Guaranty Fund, which acts as a backstop to pay claims under policies issued in that state by admitted carriers which become insolvent. This is similar to FDIC-provided insurance for certain deposits of FDIC-insured banks that become insolvent. Admitted carriers generally charge higher premiums than surplus lines carriers and have less flexibility on coverage (since, generally, all of their policies and endorsements must be state-approved except under certain "single use" exceptions) but they also provide more financial security for policyholders.

Admitted Policy

An insurance policy underwritten by an admitted carrier (see above) that has been reviewed by the insurance regulator of the state in which it is issued. The regulator reviews the form itself as well as the rating plan, which usually provides for a framework of debits and credits to the baseline price based upon a variety of factors. In the strictest sense, Admitted Policies should only be issued with state-approved endorsements, although some states allow for a one-time use exception on certain endorsements.

Actuary

Actuaries are individuals who perform a variety of analytical functions in the insurance industry. They generally possess college or advanced degrees in mathematics and/or statistical analysis. In the professional lines insurance segment, actuaries analyze various metrics to help carriers do things such as set profitable premium rates and adequate loss reserves. Actuaries who focus on premium setting are known as "Pricing Actuaries," and those who focus on analyzing loss data and setting reserves are called "Loss Actuaries" or "Reserving Actuaries."

Old insurance joke: "What's the difference between an actuary and a terrorist?"

"You can negotiate with a terrorist."

Alpha House

A term used historically to refer to the large insurance brokerages that were known colloquially by their initials of the alphabet. For example, Marsh & McLennan was "M&M," Johnson & Higgins was "J&H" and Rollins Hudig Hall was "RHH." Alpha House is still used today by industry veterans, but not nearly as much as in the days before rampant consolidation.

Around the Clock Reinstatement

A colloquial term for a reinstated limit of liability that attaches at the very top of a program – after all other layers above it have been exhausted. As an example, assume that an insured has $100 million worth of D&O Insurance limits in 10 layers of $10 million each. The primary $10 million policy contains an Around The Clock Reinstatement of the $10 million limit. If a $15 million D&O claim is paid under this program, the primary $10 million will be exhausted and the next $5 million of the claim payment will come from the policy providing the second $10 million layer of limits. The primary policy's $10 million Around the Clock Reinstatement won't attach until the remaining $85 million in limits (above the $15 million already paid) is totally exhausted. Note: This is a general illustration of the concept; the exact workings of individual policies will depend upon the specific wording involved. Also, sometimes Around the Clock Reinstatements can apply to a claim that exhausted the original limit of liability while other times they specifically do not. Again, the exact wording of the operative policy will govern how the reinstatement is applied.

Belt and Suspenders

Generally referring to something that is redundant or unnecessary, this phrase is commonly used in the insurance world in connection with exclusions in an insurance policy when one or more such exclusions are unnecessary. For example, if a D&O Insurance policy contains an exclusion for any claim brought by an officer of the insured company, an additional exclusion specifically applying to claims brought by the CEO would be considered to be Belt and Suspenders.

Beta

A number that measures the volatility of a price, usually of a stock, mutual fund or an entire portfolio, in relation to an overall market, such as the S&P 500. A Beta that's greater than 1.0 indicates that the price has fluctuated more than the overall market and a Beta below 1.0 indicates that the price has fluctuated less than the overall market. Directors and Officers Liability Insurance underwriters frequently take the Beta of a company's stock into account when analyzing that company's risk of incurring a securities class action.

B Quote

This is a quote issued by an underwriter as a favor to a broker so the broker can show his client an additional option from which to choose, although a B Quote is not intended by either the underwriter or the broker to be bound. B Quotes usually carry a higher price and/or more restrictive terms than another quote that the broker has already received in order to make it less attractive to the applicant. The practice of issuing B Quotes is unethical – and may even be illegal in many jurisdictions. Forget that you read this here.

Bad-Faith Damages

See Extra-Contractual Obligations

Black-Box Underwriting

An underwriting methodology wherein pre-set parameters are used to underwrite and quote smaller, less-complex accounts whose risk profile must fit into the "black box" established by the carrier in order to produce a quote. Accounts that don't fit into this Black Box profile are removed from the Black-Box Underwriting process as "exceptions" and are underwritten and quoted individually, or, possibly, declined altogether depending upon specific parameters of the Black Box program.

Blocking the Market

Occurs when a broker submits an account for a quote to a number of carriers with whom he doesn't intend to place the business, but rather he wants to get the submission recorded under his brokerage's name so that competing brokers can't access those carriers for quotes on that account. Generally, the first broker who submits an account to an insurer for a quote gets that account "reserved" under his firm's name (assuming that the account hasn't already been submitted to that carrier for a quote on that same line of business). Any competing brokers who then try to submit the same account for a quote on that same line of business will be "blocked out" by the first broker who made the submission.

Boilerplate Wording

A legal term used to refer to any standardized wording. In the insurance world, it's used to reference policy language (including endorsement language) that is used standardly and has not been customized or altered in any way. Compare to Manuscripted Wording below.

Book Value

When used with respect to stocks, Book Value is a method of calculating a company's overall net worth. A stock's Book Value is determined by taking the total value of a company's common stock equity and subtracting outstanding liabilities (including the value of preferred stock) and intangible assets like the value of patents and goodwill, and then dividing the result by the total number of outstanding common shares. This will yield the per-share Book Value of a company. Theoretically, if a company were to liquidate, each holder of common stock would receive the Book Value of their holdings because that would be the equity left over once debts are paid. Investors (and D&O Insurance underwriters) compare a stock's Book Value with its actual trading price to get a sense of how much the market values the company and its future prospects.

Bordereau

Any type of list in the insurance world. It is typically used to describe a list of claims that is given to the insurer at regular intervals (e.g. the Quarterly Claims Bordereau), but the term can also be used to describe lists of insureds, insurance policies or other things.

Broker of Record Letter (or "BOR")

A letter signed by someone of requisite authority evidencing the fact that a particular insurance brokerage has been chosen to represent that applicant in the process of procuring specified lines of insurance. For example, a company may give a BOR to Brokerage ABC for their D&O and E&O programs, but then give a BOR to Brokerage XYZ for their property and worker's compensation insurance programs. Broker ABC would be said to have been "BOR'ed" when a client issues a BOR to a competing broker on an insurance program that Broker ABC was previously handling. An example of what might be said in the industry: "Brokerage ABC was handling Facebook's D&O Insurance until Brokerage XYZ went in and BOR'ed it away." Some BORs will state that the change in brokers doesn't take effect for five days, in order to give the incumbent broker a chance to retain the business by persuading the client not to move his account, but this is purely a matter of custom (and courtesy) and is not generally a legal requirement.

Broker Quote or Desk Quote

A non-bindable quote that's generated by a broker without any consultation with, or the approval of, any actual underwriters. This is commonly used by brokers when trying to obtain new accounts without prior consultations with an underwriter. For example, the competing broker may say: "Carmelo, let us handle your D&O and we'll be able to get you a $25 million primary policy for only $350,000," even though the broker has no factual basis for making that statement.

Bump-Up Costs

This is a colloquial term that refers to the amount by which a company must increase the price that it offered to purchase the shares of another company. For example, Company A buys Company B for $10 a share, but disgruntled Company B shareholders sue, claiming that the company was sold too cheaply. If a court rules that Company A must pay a fair price of $12 per share for Company B, the additional $2 per share would be considered a Bump-Up Cost.

Cancel/Rewrite

This is the process of canceling an insurance policy before its natural expiration date in order to bind a new policy with the same carrier but under different terms. An example of when a Cancel/Rewrite might occur would be when an insured company makes a midterm acquisition of another company and desires higher D&O Insurance policy limits immediately. The carrier might offer to cancel the existing D&O policy on a specific date and rewrite it as a new policy going forward with the higher limits and some different terms and conditions to address any specific needs involving the acquired company.

Capacity

A carrier's ability to provide coverage for a risk, usually measured in terms of a limit of liability. For example, an underwriter might say "We have no more capacity to participate on the insured's D&O program; we've already committed a $25 million limit of liability." Another example: "Our company writes a lot of Lawyers E&O business, but we have no capacity for Medical Malpractice insurance."

Captive Insurance Company

An insurer created and owned by a parent company (usually not an insurance company, although it can be) for the purpose of insuring only the parent company's risks. Captive Insurance Companies are usually established when their parent company finds it difficult and/or unreasonably expensive to obtain insurance coverage for specific perils. Captive insurance companies can also be established to insure a group of companies within an industry. These are known as "industry captives." A Captive Insurance Company that only insures one company is known as a "pure captive." By using a Captive Insurance Company, an insured may, in certain circumstances, obtain tax and accounting benefits not available through the use of a commercial insurer. It may also receive broader coverage than otherwise possible on the open insurance market. Certain jurisdictions have created favorable laws to encourage the domicile of captive insurance companies within their borders, such as Bermuda, the Cayman Islands and Ireland overseas, and the states of Vermont, Delaware, Connecticut and Hawaii in the United States.

Captive Law Firm or Captive Counsel
A law firm whose attorneys are exclusively employees of an insurance carrier. These firms only work on cases involving insureds of their employer and do not solicit or accept assignments from the general public. Usually, captive law firms have names similar to non-captive law firms (such as The Law Offices of Nikos Diamantis, as opposed to, for example, "Insurance Carrier XYZ Captive Law Firm"), which makes it more difficult to distinguish them from non-captive firms. These firms are also sometimes called "House Counsel."

Carve-back
An exception to an exclusion, i.e. a provision that narrows an exclusion, thereby granting some measure of additional coverage. For example, if an exclusion applies to "any claim brought by one insured against another..." but it then goes on to state that the exclusion does not apply to "cross-claims, counterclaims or third-party claims between insureds," then the latter phrase would constitute a carve-back.

Cash Flow Underwriting

A process whereby an insurer will write high-risk accounts (i.e. "bad business") with the intent of collecting premium income that can then be invested and held for a period of time before it must be paid in claims arising from those high-risk accounts. The idea is to keep the cash flowing in from premiums as fast as, or faster than, the carrier must pay out the dollars in claims payments. Generally, this is how all insurers operate, but the term "Cash Flow Underwriting" is meant as a derogatory term to signify a process of writing very bad risks which don't give the carrier much time to enjoy investment income.

Cat (or Catastrophic) Cover

This is insurance coverage that usually attaches at a high level above other coverage and carries a significant limit of liability to address catastrophic losses of a large magnitude. Cat Cover can be purchased in many lines of insurance, including property (e.g. for earthquake and hurricane losses) and health (e.g. for serious illnesses or injuries). In the D&O Insurance world it is usually purchased to cover securities class actions and similar large-loss occurrences.

Claims Advocate

This is an employee of an insurance brokerage whose job is to serve as an advocate on behalf of the brokerage's clients in dealing with insurance carriers in claim situations. Claims Advocates are usually, although not always, licensed attorneys with experience as insurance company claims analysts and/or as outside coverage counsel. Almost all large insurance brokerages employ full-time Claims Advocates while many mid-sized and smaller firms do not.

Cedent

In reinsurance terms, a Cedent is an insurance company that buys reinsurance on all or a portion of a risk that it has assumed. Thus, for example, if Insurance Company XYZ writes a D&O Insurance policy with a $10 million limit of liability and then buys reinsurance for the layer of liability of $5 million in excess of $5 million, it would be a Cedent in that transaction.

Claims Arbitrage

An arrangement wherein the defendant in a pending claim buys its way out of further liability for the claim by paying a sum certain to an insurer for an insurance policy that will cover all further liability in that matter. This is akin to a loss portfolio transfer in many ways, but on a single-claim basis. An example of how this might work: Company XYZ is the defendant in a claim that it estimates will cost $12 million to resolve. In a worst-case scenario, Company XYZ could imagine the claim "blowing up" and costing as much as $20 million to resolve. Insurer ABC analyzes the claim and determines that it can dispose of it for $8 million or less. Insurer ABC offers defendant Company XYZ a deal: In exchange for a $12 million payment, Insurer ABC will assume all further responsibility for the claim. By agreeing to this offer, Company XYZ can get the claim – and its unknown future liability – off its books for a one-time payment of $12 million. If Insurer ABC manages to settle the claim for $10 million (Note: the defendant is normally required to continue cooperating with the insurer in resolving the claim after the buyout), it pockets a $2 million profit (I'll ignore frictional costs in this example). If the claim goes "pear shaped," as our British friends would say, and winds up costing $20 million, Insurer ABC would lose $8 million on the deal (again, not counting frictional costs). This is called "Claims Arbitrage" because the insurer is trying to arbitrage the difference between the sum the defendant will pay to offload the claim with certainty and the amount the insurer would then pay to resolve the claim. In the example above, Insurer ABC might write a policy covering only the one claim in question with a $20 million limit of liability (or some greater amount) for the $12 million premium payment. This may also provide some tax and accounting benefits for the defendant versus simply paying a loss outright (although, again, I emphatically do not offer any tax, legal or accounting advice in this book!)

A few important notes about Claims Arbitrage: First, the example above is only of a generic nature; there are many different ways to structure a Claims Arbitrage deal and no one definition could possibly encompass them all. Second, generally a defendant does not have to be a carrier's existing insured in order to purchase a Claims Arbitrage deal from that carrier. And third, the type of policy offered to cover the Claims Arbitrage deal does not have to be a standard insurance policy of any type; it can be totally manuscripted depending upon the circumstances.

Coinsurance

An insurance policy feature that requires the insured to retain as uninsured a certain percentage of each covered loss. There are two types of coinsurance in the American insurance market: the regular version (simply known as "coinsurance") and London-style coinsurance. See below for definition of London-style Coinsurance.

Example: Assume a D&O Insurance policy has a 10% coinsurance feature and the insured suffers a $1 million fully-covered loss. Once the 10% coinsurance is applied, the insured would receive a $900,000 recovery under the policy and would be required to bear the other $100,000 of loss itself.

Continuity

This is the concept of having an unbroken string of continual coverage in place from a specific date forward. It is most commonly used in the context of coverage for claims arising from prior acts, although it can also be used in connection with claims arising from matters underlying pending and prior claims/litigation/proceedings/investigations. A prior acts "Continuity Date" is the first date on which the insureds' acts are eligible for coverage under a policy. For example, assume that a D&O Insurance policy has a Continuity Date of Sept. 1, 2010. If a director committed a wrongful act on Aug. 15, 2010 and it gave rise to a claim against her on Dec. 1, 2010, that claim would be excluded from coverage by virtue of the Sept. 1, 2010 Continuity Date for prior acts.

A Pending and Prior Claims/Litigation/Proceedings/Investigations (it may be designated by any one or more of those terms) Continuity Date serves the same purpose, but it only excludes claims arising from claims/litigation/proceedings and/or investigations pending on or before the designated date, as well as the facts, circumstances and allegations underlying such claims/litigation/proceedings and/or investigations.

Coverage Counsel (also known as Monitoring Counsel)

A law firm hired by an insurance carrier to, among other things, conduct a coverage analysis of a claim, draft a coverage letter (see below), monitor the claim's ongoing developments and prepare status reports for the insurer. While specific duties vary from case to case (and may include one or more of the aforementioned tasks plus others), Coverage Counsel may also provide recommendations on setting reserves and may conduct settlement negotiations on behalf of the carrier.

CPCU

This is the acronym for Charted Property Casualty Underwriter, a professional designation (established in 1942) earned after successful completion of nine graduate-level courses and the passing of a rigorous test accompanying each. It is considered one of the most prestigious professional designations in the property and casualty insurance industry. Candidates must study, among other things, insurance law, risk management, contracts, liability insurance, property insurance, finance, corporate structures and ethics. CPCU designation holders are bound by a code of ethics. They must also meet experience requirements. The Chartered Property Casualty Underwriter Society has more than 150 local chapters throughout the United States.

Cut-Through Arrangement

An arrangement whereby an insurance company agrees to financially backstop an insurer with a weak financial position. The "Cut Through" allows insureds of the weak carrier to cut through to the more financially stable insurance company should they need claim payments. In essence, the Cut Through is a financial guarantee on the ability of the weak insurer to make claim payments.

Defense Outside The Limits

When a liability insurance policy's defense costs payments do not erode (i.e. are not subtracted from) the policy's overall limit of liability, the policy is said to provide a Defense Outside The Limits. Some carriers who offer this feature cap the amount of defense costs they cover outside of the policy's limits. This cap could be, for example, equal to the amount of the policy's limit of liability or some percentage thereof. Thus, if a D&O Insurance policy had a $10 million limit of liability with a Defense Outside The Limits feature, such defense costs might be capped at $10 million.

Other policies have an unlimited Defense Outside the Limits feature, although that is not common in today's insurance market. Carriers can also employ ways of limiting the application of a Defense Outside the Limits feature, such as terminating it when a settlement demand is made that is acceptable to the carrier.

Derivative Action/Derivative Lawsuit

A lawsuit brought by one or more shareholders of a company in the name of, and on behalf of, the company itself against a third party or parties. The law governing Derivative Actions varies by jurisdiction but, generally, shareholders seeking to proceed with a Derivative Action must first demand that the company itself seek redress for the grievance underlying the suit. Frequently, shareholder plaintiffs in Derivative Actions simply allege that making a demand would be futile so they've bypassed that requirement. It would be up to the court in such an instance to determine whether to waive the demand requirement.

A Derivative Action gets its name from the fact that the shareholders bringing it are deemed to have <u>derived</u> their right to bring the suit by virtue of their ownership stake in the company. Often these suits are filed against the directors and officers of a company to obtain compensation for harm they've allegedly caused the company and/or to force a specific course of action. Many jurisdictions allow (or require) a company to form a special litigation committee to investigate the allegations in the Derivative Action. This committee then decides if the company itself should bring the lawsuit or if it is meritless and should be dropped.

Derivative Actions against directors and officers are generally eligible for coverage under the "A-Side" (coverage for individual directors and officers) of a D&O Insurance policy.

Difference in Conditions ("DIC") Coverage

DIC coverage, which can be provided by endorsement or a stand-alone policy, comes in many varieties and is used not only in professional lines but also in other areas of insurance, such as property (where DIC coverage often applies to hard-to-insure perils such as earthquakes and floods). The basic concept is to provide coverage that fills in the gaps created by perils that are excluded in an underlying policy. In the world of D&O Insurance, DIC coverage normally takes the form of an excess Side A policy that's broader than the underlying Side A coverage. For example, a Side A DIC policy may drop down to serve as primary Side A coverage when the underlying policy is rescinded by the carrier. As a rule of thumb, DIC policies generally fill in gaps in underlying insurance coverage.

Discovery Period/Extended Reporting Period

A period of time after a policy's expiration during which an insured is afforded the opportunity to report claims arising from wrongful acts that occurred prior to the expiration date (and after the policy's retroactive date, if one is applicable). The right to elect a Discovery Period or Extended Reporting

Period (ERP) is explicitly set forth in the D&O Insurance policy and, frequently, the cost is predetermined and stated as well. For example, a one-year Discovery Period/ERP may cost 150 percent of the policy's annual premium and a three-year Discovery Period/ERP may cost 200 percent of the policy's annual premium.

The Discovery Period/ERP may be granted on a unilateral or bilateral basis. When granted on a unilateral basis, the insured may elect the Discovery Period/ERP only when the insurer cancels or non-renews the policy. When granted on a bilateral basis, the insured may elect the Discovery Period/ERP when either the insurer or the insured decides to cancel or non-renew the policy.

Double-Dipping

This occurs when a broker accepts a flat fee on an account placement from his client and, also, a commission on the premium from the carrier. Double-Dipping is generally not illegal if fully disclosed and agreed to by all parties. If not fully disclosed, it may be illegal or, at the very least, unethical.

Double Excess/Triple Excess Outside Directors' Liability ("ODL")

D&O policies sometimes provide coverage for insured individuals who serve as directors on the boards of outside companies. Typically, this coverage is provided on a "Double Excess" or "Triple Excess" basis. If it's provided on a Double Excess basis, the D&O policy only responds after the outside entity's D&O Insurance and the outside entity's obligation to indemnify that individual have both been exhausted. If the coverage is provided on a Triple Excess basis, then it only responds after: 1) the exhaustion of the outside entity's D&O Insurance; 2) the exhaustion of the outside entity's ability or obligation to indemnify the director; and 3) the exhaustion of the insured entity's ability to indemnify its director who was sitting on the outside board.

Duty to Defend Policy

A type of liability insurance policy that requires the insurer to assume the defense of the insured in the event of a covered claim. Typically, under a Duty to Defend Policy the insurance carrier chooses a law firm to defend the insureds against a covered claim (sometimes subject to the insureds' approval of the firm) and pays the law firm's bills directly after the self-insured retention is satisfied. As a general rule applicable in many jurisdictions, the duty to defend is broader than the duty to indemnify and, thus, a carrier may end up paying the full amount of defense costs in a covered claim but may not ultimately be obligated to pay any portion of a settlement or judgment. Most D&O Insurance policies on the market today are not Duty to Defend Policies, unlike the majority of E&O policies.

Earnings Per Share ("EPS")

A metric used as a tool in assessing the financial health of a publicly-traded company. A company's Earnings Per Share (or

"EPS") figure is determined by subtracting the company's preferred dividend payments from its net income and then dividing that result by the number of average shares outstanding over a specific period. A company's EPS is typically calculated on a quarterly and an annual basis, although other time periods can also be used.

Endorsement

An addendum to a professional lines insurance policy that alters the policy's terms and conditions. This is also called a "rider" with respect to fidelity bonds and many personal lines of insurance coverage (e.g. homeowners' insurance). Endorsements are usually, although not always, found at the end of a D&O Insurance policy.

Evergreen Endorsement

An endorsement that guarantees a policy renewal at a certain price (or with a specified cap on any increases) provided that the expiring policy has no claims reported under it (or, sometimes, no claims reserved over a certain amount or, even, no claim payments made). This type of endorsement is most common in a soft market.

Ex Gratia Payment

In Latin, Ex Gratia means "by favor." In the insurance claims world, the term refers to a claim payment that is not strictly justified by the black letter of the policy; rather, it's made in order to enhance or maintain an insurer-insured relationship.

Importantly, Ex Gratia payments are normally not covered by reinsurance (since they do not adhere to the terms of the policy that the reinsurer agreed to reinsure) thus, when a carrier makes an Ex Gratia payment, it normally comes out of the carrier's bottom line with no reinsurance offset. Most insurance carriers try to avoid making Ex Gratia payments, but they do occur on occasion.

Extended Limit

An insurance policy's limit of liability that is extended beyond its original expiration date, usually because a claim has been made under the policy – or some other situation has caused uncertainty, e.g. the announcement of a potential merger – making the insurer reluctant to commit a new limit of liability. For example, if a potentially significant claim is filed two weeks before a D&O policy's expiration, the underwriter may say to the broker, "We need to see how this claim develops. We'd like to extend the current $10 million limit for another six months before deciding on a renewal option." By doing this, the insurer restricts all claims and potential claims to one limit of liability (the Extended Limit) rather than exposing two separate limits by offering a new limit.

Extra-Contractual Obligations (ECO) or Bad-Faith Damages

Just as with any other contract, an insurance policy carries with it a duty on the part of all parties to act in good faith and engage in fair dealing. If one side breaches that responsibility, they might be acting in bad faith and could be held liable for damages in excess of whatever obligations they would otherwise have had under the policy. For example, if a carrier writes a D&O Insurance policy with a $1 million limit of liability but unfairly denies a claim while acting in bad faith, the insured could, theoretically, recover an amount far in excess of the policy's $1 million limit in a bad-faith lawsuit. This type of recovery would subject the carrier to an Extra-Contractual Obligation, or ECO, since the money it would have to pay out in excess of the $1 million policy limit would be beyond the terms of the insurance policy, thus it would be extra-contractual.

Threats of a bad-faith lawsuit are one of the most potent weapons an insured has when it believes that an insurer is not handling a claim fairly. It's important to note, however, that each state has its own bad-faith laws, and each claim turns on its particular circumstances. It's also important to note that ECO damages are generally not available in arbitration proceedings, which is why most carriers prefer to arbitrate coverage disputes with insureds rather than litigate them in court.

Facultative Reinsurance

This is reinsurance that is placed on a "one-off" basis for an individual account, as opposed to an entire portfolio of risks across the board. Also referred to colloquially in the insurance industry as "Fac." Compare with Treaty Reinsurance below.

Fee at Risk

An arrangement whereby an insurance brokerage agrees that if it can't deliver on promised coverage and/or pricing to a client (usually a new client), it will forfeit all or some percentage of its fee for the work. This inducement is sometimes made by brokerages when competing for a new client in an RFP (see below). For example, a brokerage may agree that if it can't reduce the existing premiums by 25 percent it will forfeit 50 percent of its compensation for doing the work.

File and Use

Most U.S. states require admitted insurers (see above) to submit insurance policy forms and premium rating plans to their state insurance departments for review and approval before they can be used. However, some states have a File and Use system that allows carriers to file their policy forms and/or premium rates and then immediately begin using them in that state pending the final review.

Finite Risk Insurance

This falls within the general category of non-traditional insurance products that are known as "Alternative Risk Transfer." There's an almost unlimited universe of perils that Finite Risk insurance can cover, including D&O losses and other high-severity perils, so it's included here.

At one time finite risk was a "sexy" term in the insurance industry because some finite risk deals brought in tens of millions of dollars in premiums – or even hundreds of millions of dollars (real or notional). But then, almost overnight, Finite Risk became a forbidden phrase to use in many quarters. Some deals went bad and regulators and insurance company internal audit departments increased their scrutiny of the products' structures and accounting and tax treatments. There was a strong suspicion that many of these arrangements were not true insurance transactions. Most, if not all, of the relatively small number of carriers who wrote finite risk products abandoned the line altogether by the late 1990s.

Finite risk does not have a standardly-accepted specific definition within the insurance industry, so I turned to Bob Omahne for assistance. Bob was one of the pioneers of the product and a prominent underwriter of Finite Risk Insurance during its heyday. Keep in mind that Bob's definition of Finite Risk applies to the product in its classic, unadulterated form, not the distorted version that later caused various problems. According to Bob, Finite Risk is a risk-transfer technique that combines self-funding with traditional risk transfer. One of its key elements is the spreading of an insured entity's risk over time rather than pooling the entity's risk with other insureds contemporaneously. Typical characteristics of classic Finite Risk include: 1) a multiyear term; 2) one aggregate limit of liability (sometimes with an available reinstatement option); 3) flexible/broad coverage terms; 4) a low net cost of insurance (because of profit sharing); 5) premiums based upon individual account loss experience; and 6) highly customized structures.

Follow Form or Following Form

When an insurance policy attaches in excess of an underlying policy and it conforms to all (or almost all) terms and conditions of the underlying policy, it is considered to be a "Follow Form" excess policy. A policy can be a true Follow Form excess policy that incorporates every coverage term and condition of the underlying policy (save for the limits and attachment point) or it can be generally a Follow Form policy but with specific exceptions that are noted by endorsement.

Frictional Costs

Incidental or supplemental costs, either direct or indirect, associated with an insurance transaction. Using a finite risk transaction as an example, in addition to requiring the insured to pay a $10 million premium for a $10 million limit of liability, the carrier may also assess Frictional Costs of $200,000 to cover brokerage fees, the insurer's policy issuance and claims handling costs and other expenses, plus a profit for doing the transaction.

Fronting Arrangement

When an insurance company issues a policy on its paper but is fully (or almost fully) reinsured on that risk by another insurer (and, sometimes, even by another company that is not an insurer), it's known as a Fronting Arrangement. This might be done for any number of reasons, including when the reinsuring entity doesn't have admitted paper in a particular state or when its financial rating does not meet an insured's minimum requirement, but the fronting company's financial rating does.

"Gravy" Business

A colloquialism used in the insurance world to refer to accounts that are considered very low risk and, therefore, are likely to be profitable. An example of when the term might be used: An underwriter says to a broker, "OK, I'll write this dog of an account for $100,000 even though I don't like it, but I expect you to give me $500,000 worth of gravy business within three months to make up for this."

"Hammer Clause"/Settlement Clause

Insureds and brokers colloquially (and derogatorily) refer to this provision of a D&O Insurance policy as the "Hammer Clause," while carriers use the more genteel "Settlement Clause." The purpose of this provision is to cap the insurer's liability after the point where the plaintiff has evidenced a willingness to accept a sum certain in settlement of a claim. For example, if a plaintiff agrees to accept a $1 million settlement while there is still another $4 million of limits available under the policy, a traditional Hammer Clause would cap the insurer's total liability at whatever defense costs have been expended up until that point _plus_ the $1 million that the plaintiff would have accepted to settle the case. The insured is usually allowed to continue to contest a claim beyond that point, but if the case ultimately costs more than the aforementioned total, the insured will be on the hook for the additional amount. Some Hammer Clauses in soft markets are watered-down to say that the insured will only be liable for 50 percent of the additional amount, or some other percentage less than 100 percent.

Hard Market

A colloquial term used to describe insurance market conditions that are favorable to carriers and not as favorable to insureds. Characteristics of a Hard Market include a reduced amount of available capacity in the overall market, rising premiums and more restrictive coverage terms. Hard Markets are usually triggered by significant events, such the payment of many large losses in a relatively short period of time and/or the withdrawal of insurers from the market, either through insolvency or a voluntary exit.

Increased Limits Factor ("ILF")

This is the percentage figure used to increase a quote from a base amount. For example, if a primary $5 million limit of liability is priced at $100,000 and the insured requests a quote for a $10 million limit, using an ILF of .5 would lead to a price of $50,000 for the $5 million layer in excess of the primary $5 million layer. Thus, the entire $10 million limit of liability would cost $150,000.

Indemnity Insurance Policy

An insurance policy that does not require the issuing carrier to pay defense costs as they are incurred but rather allows the carrier to indemnify the insured after the insured has paid defense costs for a covered claim (contrast with Duty to Defend Policy above). D&O Insurance policies are normally (although not exclusively) written as Indemnity Insurance Policies, however the exact terms of reimbursement may vary from carrier to carrier.

Indication

An estimate of what an actual quote might be. This is also known as a "ballpark quote." An Indication cannot be bound (unlike a quote) and is usually subject to receipt and review of additional information.

Insurance Agent

An individual who sells insurance while acting on behalf of an insurance carrier (as opposed to acting on behalf of the purchaser; compare this with **Insurance Broker** below). Insurance Agents can be employees of an insurance carrier or can be independently employed. In addition, they can be what's known as "independent agents" working on behalf of two or more insurance carriers or they can be "captive agents" working exclusively on behalf of one insurance carrier. Insurance Agents are usually authorized to perform a number of tasks on a carrier's behalf, such as offering quotes, binding policies, collecting premiums and providing administrative services such as adding cars to an auto policy. Insurance Agents generally have no duty to assess an applicant's insurance needs and assure that the proper coverage is purchased since an Insurance Agent's primary loyalty lies with the insurance carrier.

Insurance Aggregator

It's difficult to provide an exact, universally accurate definition for this term. Generally, an Insurance Aggregator is an insurance brokerage that places business that's produced (or originated) by other insurance brokerages. Those producing brokerages are usually smaller retailers that don't have an appointment with (i.e. they are not authorized to do business directly with) all of the carriers from which they'd like to receive quotes for their clients. This is usually because these smaller retailers don't have a large enough volume of business to get an appointment with a specific carrier and, even if they did, most of these small retailers wouldn't be able to fulfill the carrier's ongoing growth requirements. Hence, the Insurance Aggregator acts as a middleman to grant the retailers access to a wider variety of carriers than they would obtain on their own. The Insurance Aggregator is viewed by carriers as a single business production source (or a single appointed broker), so by aggregating accounts from small retailers, Insurance Aggregators can earn higher commission payments, including contingent payments based on overall volume, than small retailers would obtain on their own. The Insurance Aggregator can then share some portion of this increased income with individual producing retailers. Insurance Aggregators often charge annual membership dues to retailers and pursue a goal of being an important part of each small retailer's business strategy.

Carriers benefit by this arrangement because Insurance Aggregators allow them to write accounts that, in many cases, would be too expensive and/or time-consuming for them to locate.

At first blush, Insurance Aggregators may sound a lot like insurance wholesalers (see "Wholesale Broker/Wholesaler" definition below), but they differ in significant ways, including by charging membership dues. Wholesalers tend to specialize in placing more complex "one-off" risks on an "as needed" basis for their retail brokerage clients. These accounts frequently require customized policies negotiated on an individualized basis, whereas Insurance Aggregators focus on placing a high volume of less complicated accounts.

The term Insurance Aggregator is also used with respect to a somewhat different business model, brokerages that place business via the internet for individual customers seeking auto, life and other personal lines insurance coverages. In this dynamic, no originating retail broker is involved, but rather individual applicants deal directly with Insurance Aggregators on-line (or by phone) to obtain their personal lines policies.

Insurance Broker

A licensed insurance intermediary who represents a client, the insured, in placing insurance with insurance carriers. An Insurance Broker's primary loyalty lies with the client, not the carrier (as opposed to an **Insurance Agent**, defined above), and it is almost never authorized to perform any functions on the insurance carrier's behalf other than collect premiums from the insured and remit them to the carrier and, sometimes, perform tasks like issuing certificates of insurance. Also, unlike an Insurance Agent, an Insurance Broker generally has a duty to assess a client's insurance needs and procure the appropriate coverage.

Inverted Warranty

See definition of Warranty Statement/Warranty Letter below. An Inverted Warranty is a Warranty Statement that is incorporated directly into a policy form as an exclusion. Sometimes it's included as an endorsement and other times it's a provision in the policy's main section (as opposed to appearing in a separate letter or other document.) An Inverted Warranty is also sometimes known as a "Prior Knowledge Exclusion," or simply a "Knowledge Exclusion."

"Knife and Fork Man"

This is an insurance professional (not necessarily a male) who excels at client entertainment, such as hosting meals and golf outings. This person, whose job function is usually classified as "producer" or "client executive" in insurance brokerage terms, uses his advanced schmoozing skills to bring in new business and/or to retain existing accounts. This person is also sometimes said to be "all teeth and cufflinks."

Last Look

When an insurance broker gives an incumbent carrier an opportunity to review one or more quotes from competing carriers on an account before the incumbent offers its quote, the broker is said to be giving the incumbent a Last Look at the account. The idea behind this is to provide the incumbent a last chance to beat the competing quotes if it wants to retain business that may otherwise move to another carrier with a more attractive quote. If the account does move to a new carrier, the broker can say, "Hey, I gave you Last Look and you didn't step up to the plate with a good enough quote."

Laundry List

A colloquial term referring to a list of claims and/or potential claims that an insured provides to an insurer under a D&O Insurance policy's notice provision. The Laundry List is typically provided shortly before the policy's expiration and usually when the insured is moving its account to a new carrier. This is done in order to have all of the old claims classified under the expiring policy and to protect the fresh limit of liability under the new policy. In the insurance world, the term is used as both a noun and a verb. An example of its use as a verb: "ABC Corporation Laundry Listed its old carrier before moving its D&O coverage to Chubb." On occasion, the new carrier will assist the insured in crafting the Laundry List to send to the incumbent carrier so that the list is as comprehensive as possible (and, thus, as protective as possible of the new carrier's fresh limit of liability.)

Liberalization Clause

An insurance policy provision which states that if the policy form is liberalized (i.e. the coverage is broadened) in any way on a standard basis after the issuance of the policy in question, then the carrier agrees to automatically grant such broader coverage under the policy in question. For example, assume a D&O Insurance policy containing a Liberalization Clause is issued on Jan. 1, 2012 with a built-in pollution exclusion. If on March 1, 2012 the issuing carrier decides to remove the pollution exclusion from all of its D&O Insurance policies issued from that date forward, due to the presence of the Liberalization Clause that carrier would have to remove the pollution exclusion from the Jan. 1, 2012 policy. Liberalization Clauses can also be drafted to state that the insured will get the benefit of any liberalized terms granted by the carrier, even if only to one other insured and not across the board for all such policies, after the date of binding of the original policy. Liberalization Clauses can have a number of restrictions, such as, for example, only applying when the enhancement is provided for free to other insureds (thus enhancements which require an additional premium wouldn't trigger the Liberalization Clause) and only when the enhancement is given to insureds in a particular jurisdiction.

Litigation Management Guidelines

A set of guidelines that insurance carriers provide to defense counsel to govern the law firm's handling of the defense of the carrier's insured. Typically, Litigation Management Guidelines will address a variety of issues, including the maximum hourly rates that partners, associates and paralegals may charge, staffing levels (e.g. no more than one attorney may attend a deposition) and expenses (e.g. the carrier will pay no more than 10 cents per page for faxes and will only reimburse for coach-class airfare).

Lloyd's Name

An investor in a Lloyd's of London syndicate is known as a "name" (also referred to as a "member"). The capital provided by Lloyd's Names stands behind policies issued by Lloyd's syndicates to pay claims. Traditionally, only individuals were allowed to be Lloyd's Names and each faced unlimited liability – with the real possibility of losing all of their personal assets – until 1994 when Lloyd's began allowing corporate investors, with a limit on their liability. Today, any individual who becomes a Lloyd's Name also enjoys the benefit of a cap on their personal liability (although some longer tenured individual Lloyd's Names still have unlimited personal liability). Individuals comprise less than 20 percent of Lloyd's Names today, and the percentage is expected to continue shrinking over time.

Lloyd's of London

Often mistakenly thought of as an insurance company by those not in the insurance industry, Lloyd's of London is a market for insurance and reinsurance business that is underwritten by various member syndicates. It was founded at Edward Lloyd's coffee shop in London in 1688 and is the world's oldest continuously active insurance market. Lloyd's serves as a market regulator and also facilitates the business of insurance by offering administrative services. Headquartered at One Lime Street in London, Lloyd's operates under the motto of "Uberrimae fides" ("of the utmost good faith" in Latin).

London-Style Coinsurance

An insurance policy feature wherein the coinsurance percentage reduces the policy's overall limit of liability. For example, assume a policy has a 10 percent coinsurance feature and a $10 million limit of liability. Using London-Style Coinsurance the carrier would pay 90 percent of all loss (the insured being responsible for the other 10 percent) above the self-insured retention until covered loss reached the policy's $10 million limit. Thus, the carrier would pay a total of $9 million in loss before exhausting the policy. Using American-style coinsurance, the carrier would pay 90 percent of all covered loss until it paid out its full $10 million limit of liability. Thus, it would require $11 million of covered loss above the self-insured retention to exhaust the entire policy using the normal American method of calculation.

It's important to note that not all London-based insurers use London-Style Coinsurance on every policy and, as always, the specific terms and conditions of a particular policy will govern the policy's operation.

"Look-Up" Endorsement

An endorsement to a policy that affords a carrier the right to review the terms and pricing of all policies on the excess layers above its layer. This is usually requested by a carrier when it fears that insurers of layers above are enjoying more favorable terms and/or pricing than the layer written by the insurer requesting the Look-Up Endorse-ment. This is most commonly found during soft (i.e. more competitive) markets when pricing hits a minimum level at some point in an insurance program's excess layers and remains flat for the remainder of the tower. For example, when minimum rates-per-million are reached, a carrier writing $10 million in excess of $100 million may get the same rate per million as a carrier attach-ing $20 million above that level, in which case the lower attaching carrier might feel cheated for assuming more risk at the same price as the higher attaching competitor.

Loss Arbitrage

See Claims Arbitrage above.

LMU ("Loss Mitigation Unit")

This term originated at AIG in the 1990s. The Loss Mitigation Unit was a group within AIG that devised innovative ways to transfer risk, thus falling under the general umbrella of Alternative Risk Transfer products. Over time, the name of the group (and its acronym of LMU) became synonymous with the general concept of these Alternative Risk Transfer products, thus, people would say things like "They're buying an LMU for that exposure," or "We wrote three new LMUs this month." The term appears to be out of favor in today's market.

Loss Portfolio Transfer

An arrangement whereby an insurance company pays another insurer (usually a reinsurer) to assume all future liabilities for claims arising from a particular class of business the insurance company has written. For example, if Insurance Company A decides to exit the D&O market in Texas, it may do a Loss Portfolio Transfer deal (also commonly referred to as an "LPT") with Reinsurer B whereby Reinsurer B assumes responsibility for all outstanding claims under all of Insurance Company A's D&O Insurance policies written in Texas. In exchange for this, Insurance Company A will pay Reinsurer B a premium. This premium may be calculated using the aggregate amount of all expected losses in the portfolio being transferred (adjusted for time value of money) as well as additional funds for handling claims through to resolution and other assorted costs. The structure of each LPT deal turns on its own facts and usually involves a thorough audit and assessment of all outstanding claims as well as consideration of a variety of other factors.

Loss Triangle

A table of data showing losses over a specific period of time, usually depicted in years. Loss Triangles can be created for many reasons, including to show loss development for a particular insured's account or an insurer's entire portfolio of business by product line or overall. Loss triangles can show actual paid claims, losses which have been reserved for but not yet paid, or a combination thereof (with actual losses for closed-out years and projected losses for more recent and/or future years). Because there are more entries for older years and fewer data points as the table progresses toward the present, the data normally assumes the shape of a triangle, hence the name Loss Triangle.

Managing General Agent (MGA)

An insurance brokerage that's authorized to underwrite policies on behalf of an insurance carrier. Generally, the carrier will issue a "Letter of Authority" to the MGA specifying the lines of business to be written and such things as: 1) the policy form(s) to be used; 2) coverage parameters that must be maintained; 3) maximum limits of liability to be written and minimum retentions to be imposed; 4) restrictions on the size and nature of individual accounts; and 5) the maximum amount of premium that the MGA is authorized to collect annually. The preceding list is not, of course, exhaustive. An MGA's duties typically include soliciting submissions, underwriting applications, issuing quotes and declinations, binding accounts, issuing policies, collecting premiums and remitting them to the appropriate carrier and other administrative acts relating to the foregoing. Note: Brokerages that perform these functions in the life and health insurance fields are generally called Managing General Underwriters or MGUs.

Some MGAs also adjust claims on behalf of the carrier (compare with Third Party Administrator below).

MGAs are typically paid on commission by the carrier (which they deduct from premiums before remitting them), although some also receive compensation based on an insurance program's profitability. This gives the MGA incentive to write good business and not merely seek high volumes of premium to maximize commission income.

Manuscripted Wording

Customized language that has been specifically drafted to achieve a unique objective (as opposed to "Boilerplate Wording" as defined above). When an underwriter drafts an endorsement to address a specific exposure of an insured, that endorsement is said to contain Manuscripted Wording and is considered to be a "manuscripted endorsement."

Market Service Agreement (MSA) or Placement Service Agreement (PSA)

An MSA/PSA is an incentive arrangement between an insurance brokerage and an insurer that motivates the broker to place a high volume of its business with that particular carrier by increasing compensation amounts for the broker as pre-set financial goals are met. For example, a carrier may agree to pay 12 percent commission on the first $5 million of premium that a brokerage places with the carrier in a year. Then, after the brokerage reaches the $5 million mark, the commission may increase to 15 percent for the rest of the year.

MSAs/PSAs can be structured in many different ways, including flat, one-time payouts from the carrier to the brokerage for achieving a specified premium level in a year. MSAs/PSAs are sometimes colloquially referred to as "back-end compensation" for the broker.

Generally, MSAs/PSAs are not illegal, although ethical considerations dictate that their existence should be disclosed by insurance brokers to their clients in the interest of full transparency. In the mid-2000s a number of brokerage firms paid substantial fines for not disclosing to clients that they had MSAs/PSAs with insurance carriers. MSAs/PSAs continue to exist today, albeit generally with more pronounced and comprehensive disclosure to clients than in years past.

Mid-Term Quote

A quote that would take effect sometime before the natural expiration date of an in-force policy. For example, if a D&O Insurance policy was effective from Jan. 1, 2010 to Jan. 1, 2011 and a competing carrier issued a quote to that insured with a proposed inception date of May 1, 2010, that would be a Mid-Term Quote. Note: A Mid-Term Quote doesn't have to take effect at the exact midpoint of the existing in-force policy, just any time before the policy's natural expiration date. Most carriers decline to issue Mid-Term Quotes unless there are extenuating circumstances (e.g. the incumbent carrier is teetering on insolvency and all its insureds start seeking coverage elsewhere). One justification I've heard for carriers eschewing Mid-Term Quotes is that carriers are busy enough quoting their renewals and new-line submissions and if they were forced to start quoting and defending accounts mid-term, it would create a lot of extra work and cause chaos in the market.

North American Industry Classification System (NAICS)
See **SIC Code** definition below.

Naive Capacity
A derogatory insurance colloquialism applied to carriers that are not knowledgeable and/or experienced in a particular line of business. For example, an auto insurance carrier that decides to delve into the D&O Insurance market and begins writing primary layers on difficult risks for low premiums would be considered to be offering Naive Capacity.

Oversubscribed
When more carriers than are needed would like to provide capacity for a particular insurance program it is said to be Oversubscribed.

Panel Counsel
A law firm that is on a list (or "panel") of firms approved by an insurer to defend insureds in covered claims under the insurer's policies. Sometimes insureds are given the opportunity to choose their defense counsel from a list of Panel Counsel law firms, while other times the insurance carrier

unilaterally appoints defense counsel from the Panel Counsel list. The specific procedure depends upon the terms of the applicable insurance policy. Under a "duty to defend" insurance policy, the carrier normally chooses the defense counsel for a claim while under a "reimbursement" insurance policy, which is the most popular type of D&O Insurance policy on today's market, the insured is allowed to pick a law firm to defend it, but that firm must still be approved by the carrier to work on the claim.

Part Of or P/O

When a carrier provides a limit of liability on an insurance program that is part of an overall larger layer, it's said to be "Part Of" and often memorialized in writing with the shorthand "P/O." For example, if Carrier ABC and Carrier XYZ each provide a $10 million limit of liability within an overall $20 million layer of insurance limits, then each is said to be writing "$10 million Part Of $20 million." This might also be written in insurance shorthand as "$10 million P/O $20 million." See Quota Share or Co-Surety below.

PEG Ratio (Price-Earnings to Growth Ratio)

The PEG Ratio attempts to measure a stock's current value and future growth prospects. The PEG Ratio is calculated by dividing a stock's P/E Ratio (see below) by the company's earnings-per-share growth rate over a specific period. When calculating the PEG Ratio, one can use either historical growth rates, which would yield what's known as "the trailing PEG," or future growth projections, known as the "forward PEG." As a general rule, although there are exceptions, especially for certain industries, a PEG Ratio below 1.0 indicates an undervalued company and a PEG Ratio above 1.0 indicates an overvalued company. The PEG Ratio is considered by many to be a more valuable metric to value a stock than Earnings Per Share (EPS) or the Price-Earnings Ratio (P/E).

P/E Ratio (Price-Earnings Ratio)

A metric used to judge the relative value of a stock's price. The P/E Ratio is calculated by dividing the current market price of a stock by the earnings per share (EPS; defined above). For example, if Company XYZ's stock was trading at $55 per share and the earnings per share over the past four quarters was $5, the P/E (known as the "trailing P/E" because it takes into account past earnings, not future earnings projections) for the stock would be 11 (55 ÷ 5). The P/E Ratio is also commonly known as a stock's "earnings multiple," "price multiple" or, simply, "multiple." As a general rule, although there are exceptions, companies with higher P/E Ratios than competitors in the same space are seen as more attractive by the investing public. It's important, however, to compare P/E Ratios between companies within the same industry and even, sometimes, the same specific niche within an overall industry, because average P/E Ratios can vary by industry and can vary by niches.

Pre-Booking

Largely a historical term – and included here mainly for nostalgic reasons – Pre-Booking was the name given to the practice of insurance carriers recognizing premium revenue before an account was actually bound. Accounts were sometimes Pre-Booked so an insurer could meet its revenue goals for the month – even though sometimes those Pre-Booked numbers would later be "backed out" at the beginning of the next month when the account failed to bind. Stepped-up regulatory enforcement and a general tightening of business standards in the early- and mid-2000s put an end to Pre-Booking in virtually every (although perhaps not <u>absolutely every</u>) insurance organization. This practice was also known as "bulking" at some insurance companies (as in "booking all of the accounts in bulk").

Placement Service Agreement (PSA)

See Market Service Agreement above.

PLUS

This acronym stands for "Professional Liability Underwriting Society," a professional organization founded in 1986 by Angelo Gioia to promote education and professional development in the field of professional lines insurance. PLUS has more than 6,000 members and sponsors a number of educational conferences and other events each year. It also provides the curriculum and confers degrees for the RPLU designation (see RPLU below).

Producer

A term referring to an insurance broker who brings in, or "produces," business. Brokers who focus on negotiating and placing policies for existing clients with insurers are sometimes known as "placement" brokers, while brokers who spend their time trying to bring in new clients and also in dealing directly with existing clients are known as Producers. There is no standard model in the industry, and many individual brokers, especially at smaller brokerage firms, perform placement and Producer functions.

Program Business

A group of accounts that can be written on a "program basis," meaning they are all sufficiently similar in size (usually small) and risk characteristics so they can be underwritten on a blanket basis using Black-Box Underwriting methods.

Quota Share or Co-Surety

An arrangement whereby two or more insurance carriers share the risk on a single layer of insurance according to agreed-upon percentages. This is most commonly done on excess layers, but can also be done on primary layers. An example would be where Carrier A assumes $4 million of liability, Carrier B assumes $3 million of liability and Carrier C assumes $3 million of liability of a $10 million layer of coverage in excess of a primary $10 million layer. This would be expressed in writing, with respect to Carrier A, as "Carrier A writes $4 million P/O (insurance shorthand for "part of") $10 million XS

241

(insurance shorthand for "in excess of") $10 million. Each carrier in a quota share arrangement pays their percentage share of every claim dollar paid. Thus, if a $1,000 claim were paid in this example, Carrier A would pay $400 and Carriers B and C would be on the hook for $300 each.

Reciprocal

An unincorporated entity that acts as a de facto insurer, formed by two or more organizations or individuals, for the purpose of sharing each other's risks of a similar nature. For example, a group of securities broker/dealer firms may get together to self-fund a Reciprocal to provide Broker/Dealer E&O Insurance for each member firm and their registered representatives. The Reciprocal's capital may come solely from contributions from members (also called "subscribers") or can be comprised of a combination of member capital and outside reinsurance.

Regional Broker

A diplomatic term used to refer to an insurance brokerage that does not have national reach. Even if a brokerage has only one small office, many carriers will refer to the firm as a Regional Broker.

Reinstated Limit of Liability

This one sounds simple enough, and it generally is, although there can be twists. In its basic form, a Reinstated Limit of Liability is simply a restoration of a policy's limit of liability after the original amount has been depleted by claim payments. Generally, carriers only agree to reinstate a limit of liability on a multiyear policy, with the thought being that if a single-year policy becomes exhausted by claim payments before its expiration, the insured would be required to buy a new one-year policy (at a much higher premium, of course!) Some Reinstated Limits attach automatically when the original limit of liability is exhausted, while others only attach after the insured elects the reinstatement and pays an additional premium. Also, where one or more layers of coverage exist above the primary policy, the primary's limits usually reinstate "around the clock," (See Around the Clock Reinstatement above) meaning they attach only after all other layers of coverage above the primary have been exhausted by claim payments. Theoretically, the Reinstated Limit of Liability could attach above the original limit of liability and below any excess coverage, but this rarely happens. Also, carriers usually mandate that the Reinstated Limit of Liability does not apply to any claim that was paid (or even pending but not yet paid) under the original limit of liability.

Reinsurance Broker

An insurance broker who handles reinsurance transactions between an insurance company (the "cedent") and a reinsurer. Aon Benfield, Guy Carpenter and Willis Re are among the largest and most well-known Reinsurance Brokers.

Request for Proposal (RFP)

In the commercial insurance world, an RFP is the process whereby an insured solicits proposals from prospective insurance brokers – and usually the incumbent broker, as well – seeking to handle the insured's account. Normally, the insured issues a written RFP document to a specific set of insurance brokerages it has selected to compete for its business. This document sets forth the line(s) of business involved and usually requests specific information from the interested brokerages (e.g. resumes of all individuals who would work on the account, a list of current clients of a similar nature, projected insurance program structures and costs, etc.). Many times, although not always, the RFP process includes a personal meeting wherein the competing brokers will discuss with the prospective client various aspects of their RFP response, including their qualifications and insurance program ideas. Note: RFPs occur in many other industries as well with respect to procurement of other services and products.

Retail Insurance Broker or Retailer

An insurance brokerage that deals directly with insureds, who are their clients, and insurers (compare this with Wholesale Broker/Wholesaler below) with no middleman involved. Among the most well-known Retail Insurance Brokerages in the United States are Aon, Arthur J. Gallagher, Lockton, Marsh and Willis.

Retro (or Retroactive) Date

A date on which coverage first takes effect. The most common use of a Retro Date in D&O Insurance occurs with respect to coverage for acts committed on or after a specified date. For example, if a D&O Insurance policy has a Retro Date of Jan. 1, 2010, coverage under that policy will not apply to claims arising from wrongful acts that occurred before that date (including, usually, interrelated wrongful acts that first occurred before the Retro Date and continued after it). A Retro Date can also apply to pending and prior litigation, administrative or regulatory proceedings and investigations (e.g. an EEOC proceeding). An example of this would be when a D&O Insurance policy states that it will not apply to any claims arising from, or related to, litigation, administrative or regulatory proceedings or investigations pending on or before a specified Retro Date. Most policies will also exclude claims arising from acts, errors or omissions alleged in such pending or prior litigation, administrative or regulatory proceedings or investigations. The concept underlying a Retro Date is that the insurer doesn't want to cover "the burning building;" that is, if a problem had already occurred before the insurer came on risk, it wouldn't want to pay claims for such known situations.

Retro Date Inception ("RDI")

A term used to signify that a policy provides no coverage for claims arising from acts that took place prior to the policy's inception date. See Retro Date above.

Rider

See definition of Endorsement above.

Risk Manager

A person whose job it is to oversee the insurance purchasing and other insurance-related activities of a company. If a company is large enough, it will usually have one or more individuals solely dedicated to the insurance purchasing function. In smaller companies, the Risk Manager function may be performed by another executive, such as the chief financial officer, treasurer or general counsel. Financial institutions often designate the holder of this position as the "Insurance Risk Manager" to distinguish them from other risk managers within the company, such as those who deal with things like interest rate risk or counterparty credit risk.

Risk Purchasing Group

A group of insureds with similar risk profiles who unite to purchase insurance for all group members from a commercial insurer pursuant to the U.S. federal law known as the Liability Risk Retention Act of 1986. Risk Purchasing Groups are generally formed to enable members to obtain more favorable pricing and coverage terms from insurers than they would be able to secure individually since they are, as a group, paying a larger premium than members would pay individually (operating on the age-old retailing concept of a volume discount).

Risk Retention Group

Authorized by the U.S. federal law known as the Liability Risk Retention Act of 1986, a Risk Retention Group is an insurance company formed by members/owners engaged in the same, or similar, business activities. The Risk Retention Group's function is to provide liability insurance to the members of the group; no outside business can be accepted. Members must be businesses or governmental entities, including individual professionals such as doctors and lawyers (but not individual persons who are not insuring their professional activities), and they can only write liability coverage (not, for example, property insurance or workers' compensation insurance). The Act requires Risk Retention Groups to organize as an insurance company under the laws of at least one state (either as a captive or as a mutual insurer), but after that is accomplished, they can obtain licenses to operate in other states as well.

RPLU

This acronym stands for Registered Professional Liability Underwriter, a professional designation conferred upon individuals by the Professional Liability Underwriting Society (PLUS). It's the only professional designation in the insurance industry that is specific to professional lines underwriting. In order to earn this designation, individuals must read (through a self-study program) a total of eight PLUS Curriculum Core Modules and five PLUS Curriculum Elective Modules and pass 12 exams. Candidates must also have at least two years of experience in the professional lines insurance field in order to be eligible to earn the RPLU designation.

Run-Off Policy

An insurance policy that only covers claims arising from wrongful acts that occurred prior to the inception date of the policy. In the D&O world, run-off policies are most frequently (although not exclusively) purchased just before a company goes out of business or is acquired. The run-off policy usually provides a separate – and unimpaired – limit of liability to protect the directors and officers against claims first made during a pre-determined period of time after the former company no longer exists (in instances where the insured company is going away). Most run-off policies have a duration of either one, three or six years. Six years is generally equal to the longest statute of limitations for most civil wrongs that could be covered under a D&O Insurance policy. As a general rule, run-off D&O Insurance policies are very profitable for insurance carriers, probably because most people with high-value claims against a company don't wait until after the company is dissolved or acquired to first make their claims.

Self-Liquidating Policy (also known as a "Wasting Policy" or "Cannibalizing Policy")

When defense costs and related fees paid under an insurance policy erode the policy's overall limit of liability, it's known as a Self-Liquidating Policy or, also, a Wasting Policy or a Cannibalizing Policy. The vast majority (if not all) of the D&O

Insurance policies on the market today are written on this basis. Compare this with a Defense Outside The Limits policy (above).

Severability of the Application

A concept whereby representations made in a D&O Insurance policy's application are deemed "severable" as between insureds. This means that only certain individuals are held responsible for the application's accuracy (e.g. only those who knew the truth about misrepresentations made in the application) and only misrepresentations made by, or known by, specified executives, usually the CEO, president and CFO, will be attributed to the corporate entity for purposes of rescission or otherwise. Thus, innocent insureds are "severed" from liability with respect to these misrepresentations and will not, therefore, have the D&O policy rescinded with respect to them. Note: This definition is extremely general and is only intended to provide a basic understanding of how Severability of the Application works. There can be many variations on the above. For example, some carriers expand the list of individuals whose knowledge can negate coverage for the corporate entity to executives beyond just the CEO, president and CFO (e.g. the general counsel and the risk manager may be added.) As with all statements made in this book, specific insurance policy language must be consulted to determine how a particular policy functions.

Severability of the Exclusions

There are two general categories of exclusions in most D&O policies. One is called the "Personal Conduct Exclusions" and the other lacks a specific name, but I'll call them "General Corporate Exclusions" for our purposes. The Personal Conduct Exclusions entail such things as fraud, personal profit or gain and knowledge of prior wrongful acts. By making these Personal Conduct Exclusions severable, carriers are saying that the wrongful acts or knowledge of one insured won't be imputed to other insureds. So, for example, if one director commits fraud that's excluded by the D&O policy, he won't negate coverage for the other insureds if the policy grants Severability of the Exclusions. Essentially, the carrier is saying that the acts of one individual insured are severed from applying to any other insured.

Sharpen Your Pencil

A term used by insurance brokers to convey to underwriters that they need to reduce their premium on an account. The visual imagery is meant to suggest that by reducing the lead in their pencil to a finer point, underwriters will be able to arrive at a reduced premium calculation.

Short Rate Refund

A method of calculating a premium refund when an insured cancels an insurance policy. This method of calculation is more favorable to the insurer than a strict *pro rata* method of calculation would be. In essence, a Short Rate Refund (sometimes called an Old Short Rate) imposes a penalty on the insured for canceling the policy before its natural expiration. Some of this penalty amount is justified by carriers as being costs associated with issuing a policy and other administrative tasks. A 10 percent Short Rate penalty (beyond the pro rata amount) is typical, although in some states insurance companies are permitted to establish their own Short Rate Refund schedules.

Side A

The traditional (and colloquial) name of the insuring agreement in a D&O Insurance policy that creates coverage for directors and officers when they incur loss in connection with a covered claim that cannot be reimbursed by the corporate entity insured, either because reimbursement is prohibited by law (and/or bylaws of the company) or because the company is financially unable to provide it. Today's policies use a variety of designations for this section, including "Insured Person Coverage," "Management Liability," Directors and Officers Insurance" and "Executive Liability Coverage," as well as other names.

Side B

The traditional (and colloquial) name of the insuring agreement in a D&O Insurance policy that creates coverage to reimburse the corporate entity insured after it has indemnified individual directors and officers for covered loss in connection with a claim. Today's policies use a variety of designations for this section, including "Company Reimbursement," "Indemnification of Insured Person Coverage," "Corporate Liability Arising from Indemnifiable Loss" and "Executive Indemnification Coverage," as well as other names.

Side C

The traditional (and colloquial) name of the insuring agreement developed in 1995 to protect the corporate entity under a D&O Insurance policy against liability that it incurs on its own behalf – apart from the liability of individual directors and officers – in connection with securities claims. By creating this coverage, insurers hoped to avoid the sometimes bitter and protracted allocation disputes that would arise with insureds over what percentage of a securities claim was covered (because it was directed against individual insureds) and what percentage was not covered (because it was directed against the corporate entity). Today's policies use a variety of designations for this section, including "Company Securities Liability," "Organization Coverage," "Entity Securities Coverage" and "Corporate Liability Arising From Securities Claims," as well as other names. It's important to note that in private company D&O Insurance policies, as well as in some D&O Insurance policies for publicly-traded companies, Side C or Entity Coverage can extend to other types of claims beyond securities matters.

SIC Code

An SIC (Standard Industrial Classification) Code is a four-digit number appearing in the U.S. Office of Management and Budget's Standard Industrial Classification Manual to identify the type of business(es) in which companies engage. A single company can be classified with more than one SIC Code if it engages in a variety of business functions. D&O Insurance carriers have historically used SIC Codes to classify applicants for underwriting purposes.

The North American Industry Classification System (NAICS), established in 1997 and intended for use in the United States, Mexico and Canada, was created to supplant the SIC Code system using a more detailed and flexible structure that employs as many as six digits (although sometimes fewer) to identify businesses with more specificity than the SIC Code. The NAICS (pronounced "nakes") is intended to provide more uniformity in classifying North American businesses across national borders while also offering a superior ability to adapt to new classes of business as economies and companies evolve. However, not all organizations have converted to use of the NAICS yet, particularly insurers, and it appears that the SIC Code will continue to be relevant for some time.

Soft Market

A colloquial term used to describe insurance market conditions that are favorable to insureds and not as favorable to carriers. Characteristics of a Soft Market include an abundant amount of available capacity in the overall market, decreasing premiums and broader coverage terms. Many carriers offer multiyear policies in a Soft Market in order to offset decreasing premium rates with larger multiyear premiums (a short-term solution to generate premium growth). Soft Markets are usually arrived at gradually as premium rates slowly erode due to a variety of factors, including the entrance of new carriers to the market and favorable loss results in the market segment as a whole.

State Amendatory

An endorsement that is required to be appended to a policy by state insurance law. These types of mandatory endorsements usually expand or further protect the rights of insureds. For example, a State Amendatory might prescribe a minimum period of advance notice that a carrier must provide before canceling a policy. So, for instance, if the boilerplate language of a D&O Insurance policy calls for 30 days advance notice before the carrier may cancel the policy, a state amendatory may require at least 60 days advance notice of cancellation.

State Guaranty Fund/State Insolvency Fund

A pool of money collected by a state as a backstop to pay claims in the event that a carrier admitted in that state becomes insolvent. A Guaranty Fund is normally financed through a tax on admitted policies written in the state (usually ranging from 1 percent to 3 percent of each admitted policy's total premium). The presence of a Guaranty Fund is an incentive for insureds to place their business with admitted carriers, as opposed to surplus lines carriers, although, in reality, most state Guaranty Funds would only be able to pay a small percentage of each claim should an admitted carrier default on all of its claims obligations.

"Subject To" or Subjectivities

An insurance carrier sometimes binds an account on a temporary basis while awaiting review and approval of additional information or other items, such as a signed application. These are referred to as "Subjectivities" in insurance parlance and the policy is said to be bound "Subject To" the receipt, review and acceptance of them. Carriers may bind a policy temporarily with a specified date on which the binder (and policy) will expire if the Subject To materials haven't been received and approved. Although not common, on occasion an insurer may receive the Subject To information and not approve it, in which case the binder would expire or be canceled after some reasonable period of notice. In general, however, a carrier will not bind a policy with Subjectivities unless it is reasonably certain that the forthcoming information will be acceptable when received.

Sunset Clause

A provision in an insurance or reinsurance policy establishing a cut-off date, usually sometime after the policy's expiration, after which no notices of claim will be accepted under the policy. Extended reporting period clauses (or discovery period clauses) in D&O Insurance policies are not technically considered Sunset Clauses although they serve the same function. Sunset Clauses are typically found in occurrence insurance policies (e.g. Comprehensive General Liability Insurance) and reinsurance policies/treaties.

Surplus Lines Insurance Carrier/Non-Admitted Insurance Carrier

An insurance carrier that does business on a "non-admitted basis" in a state, meaning it has not had its policy forms and rates reviewed and approved by the state's insurance regulatory body before offering its policies for sale in that state. Such Surplus Lines Insurance Carriers are, however, still subject to each state's review for financial stability, adequacy of sales practices and other issues before they will be approved to write business in that state. These insurers are also sometimes referred to as "non-standard carriers" or "excess and surplus ("E&S") carriers" which are said to be doing business in the "non-standard market" or "E&S market." Because these insurers are not subject to the more rigid rules that govern admitted carriers, they can be more flexible in providing coverage. Sometimes Surplus Lines Insurance Carriers provide the only insurance option for higher-risk insureds. In order to place coverage with a Surplus Lines Insurance Carrier, an insurance broker must have a surplus lines broker's license and, in some states, the broker must obtain a certain number of declinations (typically three) from admitted carriers before she's able to place her client's business with a Surplus Lines Insurance Carrier. Surplus Lines

Insurance Carriers do not pay any percentage of their premiums into state insurance guaranty funds (with a limited exception in New Jersey), so if they become insolvent, there is no state-provided backstop to pay claims, unlike with admitted carriers.

Surplus Lines Insurance Policy

An insurance policy written by a surplus lines insurance carrier that is not subject to rate-and-form review by a state's insurance regulatory body. Because of this, surplus lines insurance carriers can be more flexible with the coverage they provide in a Surplus Lines Insurance Policy. For example, a surplus lines insurer can tailor endorsements to an insured's specific needs without the requirement of obtaining prior regulatory review and approval of each endorsement. However, surplus lines insurance carriers do not participate in state insurance guaranty funds (with a limited exception in New Jersey), thus if they become insolvent and are unable to pay claims under a Surplus Lines Insurance Policy, no government-provided backstop will be available to pay the insured's claims.

Third-Party Administrator (TPA)

A Third-Party Administrator ("TPA") is an outside organization that handles claims on behalf of an insurance carrier or a self-insured client on an outsourced basis. So, for example, Insurance Company A may retain Smith & Jones TPA Services, Inc., to handle all of its non-profit D&O claims. TPAs typically do things that an insurance carrier's in-house Claims Department would do, such as receive initial notices of claims (as usually set forth in the issued policies), draft coverage correspondence, select defense counsel and negotiate claim settlements. A carrier ceding authority to a TPA will normally provide the TPA with written claims handling guidelines to which it must adhere, along with specific claim settlement authority levels.

Toast

A colloquial term used to refer to policy whose limit of liability has been (or will be) totally exhausted by claim payments. An example of how it might be used in a sentence: "Damn, that policy is toast thanks to those 10b-5 claims." Toast can also be used as a verb: "That big merger claim toasted the entire D&O program, starting with the primary layer and burning through all the excess coverage." One might also say that the policy limit itself is "Toast," as in "We can write off that excess $25 million, it's toast at this point."

Treaty Reinsurance

A form or reinsurance that covers a general class of business on a blanket basis, subject to specific terms and conditions, without the need for the reinsurer to individually underwrite and approve each risk. For example, a carrier might purchase Treaty Reinsurance to reinsure 80 percent of the primary layer of liability on all non-profit D&O Insurance business that it writes up to a maximum of a $5 million primary layer per account. If the insurer were to write limits of greater than $5 million, it would have to place another treaty for those excess limits or seek facultative reinsurance (see above). Treaties normally have specific underwriting guidelines, and if a carrier wants to bind an account that doesn't meet those guidelines, it has to submit the risk to the reinsurer for individual underwriting – known as a "treaty exception" if granted.

Underwriting Cycle

The progression of the insurance market between being "hard" (i.e. rising premium rates, reduced capacity and tighter coverage terms) and "soft" (i.e. decreasing premium rates, increased capacity and more liberal coverage terms) in a cyclical manner. In general, soft-market cycles last longer than hard-market cycles. On a long-term overview chart of market conditions, hard markets normally appear as spikes between prolonged soft-market periods.

Underwriting Worksheet

A form that underwriters use to record and assess key risk metrics of an applicant. Many risk factors are usually taken into account on an Underwriting Worksheet. When assessing a publicly-traded company, for example, the Underwriting Worksheet may contain information about the company's 52-week high and low stock prices, total market capitalization, stock analysts' ratings and loss history. Depending upon the particular insurer, an Underwriting Worksheet may also be used to calculate the premium to be quoted (assuming a quote is issued as opposed to a declination) or the premium may be calculated via a separate rating worksheet or rating program (also known as a "rater").

Vanishing Deductible

A concept whereby a policy's deductible (or Self-Insured Retention/SIR) is reduced after each year for which no claim is made. So, for example, if a D&O Insurance policy begins with a $100,000 SIR in year one and no claims are filed in that year, the SIR may be reduced to $80,000 for year two under a Vanishing Deductible arrangement. If no claims are filed in year two, the SIR may be further reduced to $50,000 for year three. This concept has become popular among personal lines insurers in recent years, especially with respect to auto insurance.

Vented Layers/Corridor Retention

When an insured buys two or more layers of insurance coverage with one or more intervening layers of self-insurance, it is known as having Vented Layers of coverage and any self-insured intervening layer is called a Corridor Retention. An example of this would be where an insured buys a $10 million limit primary D&O Insurance policy, self-insures the second $10 million layer of liability and then purchases a $10 million policy in excess of the first $20 million of limits and self-insurance. That middle $10 million layer would be the Corridor Retention, and the top $10 million limit of liability would be known as a Vented Layer. This is not a common structure, but for various reasons (which would probably put you to sleep to recount), it does occur on occasion.

Void Ab Initio

Ab Initio means "from the beginning" in Latin and the phrase "Void Ab Initio" is a legal term used to describe something that was never legally valid but, rather, void right from the beginning. For example, if an insurance policy was procured through fraudulent means (e.g. with the use of false information on the policy's application), the insurance carrier may try to rescind the policy, asserting that it was Void Ab Initio because a legally binding agreement was never created due to deception on the applicant's part.

Warranty Statement / Warranty Letter/ Inverted Warranty

A statement, either incorporated into an insurance application or written as a separate letter/document, in which applicants for insurance warrant a particular fact or facts, usually that they know of no facts, circumstances or situations which may (or "are reasonably likely to," as some warranty statements say, or some variation thereof) give rise to a claim under the proposed policy. When this affirmation is built in to a policy's language, either in the body of the policy or by endorsement, it's known as an "Inverted Warranty" (see Inverted Warranty above). In such a case, the person or persons warranting the particular facts need not sign any statement but rather language is used along the lines of "[I]t is hereby understood and agreed that no person covered under this policy is aware of any fact, circumstance or situation which reasonably be expected to give rise to a claim under this policy...."

White List

A list created by some state insurance regulators (in what's known as "White List States") to designate which surplus lines carriers can write insurance products in that state.

Wholesale Insurance Brokerage/ Wholesaler

Sometimes known as a "broker's broker," a Wholesale Insurance Brokerage acts as an intermediary between retail insurance brokers (who deal directly with insurance buyers) (see Retail Broker above) and insurers. Generally, retail insurance brokers use a Wholesale Insurance Brokerage when they lack the expertise to procure the best coverage for their client in a particular product line and/or they desire capacity from an insurance company that won't deal with them for some reason, including insurance carriers who only deal with Wholesalers (such insurance companies are known as "wholesale markets.") Wholesale Insurance Brokerages frequently deal with surplus lines insurance carriers (see definition above), although they also do business with admitted carriers (see definition above). Managing general agents (see definition above) are normally organized as Wholesale Insurance Brokerages, although they differ from most Wholesalers in that they represent the interests of an insurance carrier, and have the authority to bind business on behalf of the carrier, while a traditional Wholesale Insurance Brokerage's primary allegiance lies with the retail insurance broker and its client, the insurance buyer. Insurance carriers typically pay higher commissions to Wholesale Insurance Brokerages because Wholesalers share some portion of their income on each account with the producing retail insurance broker.

Wish List

A colloquial term for a list of policy enhancements that a broker requests from a carrier in order to broaden a policy's coverage. A Wish List might request the deletion of one or more exclusions and changes to the wording of one or more provisions of the policy, such as the broadening of a definition to include more individuals as insureds.

X-Date

A shorthand reference for a policy's expiration date. Also called the "expiry" date in Canada and other English-speaking countries outside of the United States.

XS

Insurance shorthand for "excess" or "in excess of." An example would be where a broker sends an email to an underwriter stating: "Our client is looking for a $10 million-layer XS $20 million XS the primary $20 million. Will you quote?"

About the Charities

The six charities listed below will each get 15 percent of the author's share of the profits generated by this book's sales. Each charity serves a very worthy cause and we urge you to consider providing additional support on your own, whether financially or through volunteer efforts.

Go Campaign – GO Campaign identifies deserving Local Heroes throughout the world and partners with these grassroots organizations to provide children and young adults with critical services, resources and needed opportunities. It offers support and raises awareness about these small, highly-impactful organizations that might not otherwise come to the public's attention. For more information, please visit www.gocampaign.org.

Lighthouse International – Since 1905, Lighthouse International has led the charge in the fight against vision loss through prevention, treatment and empowerment. It was selected to benefit from the proceeds of this book because of the support it has provided to Arianna Collura, the daughter of Kim and Sal Collura and loving sister of Angelo and Anthony (and whose favorite uncle happens to be the author of this book). For more information, please visit www.lighthouse.org.

The Carolyn Sullivan Memorial Foundation – The Carolyn Sullivan Memorial Foundation was created in loving memory of Carolyn Sullivan - a beautiful eight year old girl who lost her battle with a brain tumor in September of 2009. The Carolyn Sullivan Memorial Foundation was started not only to keep Carolyn's memory alive, but to bring a measure of love, comfort, and support to children and families facing similar challenges associated with a chronic illness or a devastating diagnosis. It is the mission of the foundation to "pay forward" some of the love and support Carolyn's family received during her illness. The CSMF is a registered 501(c)(3) not for profit charity. For more information, please visit www.CarolynSullivanMF.com or "like" the CSMF on Facebook.

The Danielle Kousoulis Memorial Scholarship Fund – Danielle Kousoulis was working for Cantor Fitzgerald on the 104th floor of the North Tower at the World Trade Center on September 11th, 2001, and lost her life that day when terrorists flew jet airliners into the buildings. The Danielle Kousoulis Memorial Scholarship Fund was formed to continue Danielle's spirit of caring and generosity. Each year the scholarship fund awards academic scholarships to a Haddon Township (NJ) High School graduate (Danielle's alma mater; she was also a graduate of Villanova University), and to a member of Danielle's church, St. Thomas Greek Orthodox Church. As the Fund grows, it hopes in the future to also award scholarships to children of other September 11th victims. For more information, please visit www.daniellekousoulisfund.org.

The National Kidney Foundation - The National Kidney Foundation is the leading organization in the U.S. dedicated to the awareness, prevention and treatment of kidney disease for hundreds of thousands of healthcare professionals, millions of patients and their families, and tens of millions of Americans at risk. This organization was chosen for its support of Gabrielle Santiago, the wonderful daughter of Ray and Nadine Santiago (and loving big sister to Anna) who has undergone two successful kidney transplants. For more information, please visit www.kidney.org.

The St. Baldrick's Foundation – The St. Baldrick's Foundation is a volunteer-driven charity committed to funding the most promising research to find cures for childhood cancers and to give survivors long, healthy lives. It was founded by three insurance industry executives and continues to enjoy significant support from the insurance industry. For more information, please visit http://www.stbaldricks.org

About the Author

Larry (Lazarus) Goanos is the founder of Andros Risk Services LLC, an independent insurance consulting firm that offers a wide variety of services, including training for underwriters, brokers and claims professional, reviewing and critiquing insurance programs, conducting underwriting and claims portfolio audits and acting as an expert witness in insurance disputes. Larry is a graduate of Red Bank (N.J.) Catholic High School, Villanova University and Boston College Law School. He practiced law for five years at firms in New York and Boston before holding senior management positions at AIG, Marsh, ACE and Houston Casualty. You can reach Larry by email at lgoanos@androriskservices.com.

Printed in Great Britain
by Amazon